Appointment
With Death

YOUTH FORUM SERIES

A Youth Forum Book

Appointment With Death

by Alvin N. Rogness

THOMAS NELSON INC.
Nashville & New York

Library of Congress Catalog Card Number: 76–39592
ISBN: 0–8407–5319–5

Printed in the United States of America

Foreword

This book is one of a series in a unique publishing effort in which Youth Research Center, Inc., Minneapolis, Minnesota, has joined with Thomas Nelson Inc., Camden, New Jersey. The books are based on the very real concerns, problems, aspirations, searchings and goals of young people today as measured by the research center.

Central to the series is the belief that we all have a compelling need to turn to a core of faith for guidelines in coping with the world in which we live. Each book deals with a specific need or concern of young people viewed in relation to the Christian faith. By drawing upon the results of the surveys, each author is helped to speak more directly to the conflicts, values and beliefs of today's young people.

The significance of this series is enhanced, as well, by the scholarship and commitment of the authors. The grasp of the field in which each writes lends authority to their work and has established this series as a basic reference eagerly read and appreciated by young people.

Table of Contents

Preface

Grief came suddenly to our house at 10:10 P.M. the night of August 18, 1960.

Throughout the dinner hour we had awaited our second son, Paul, 24, who had just completed two years at Pembroke College, Oxford, as a Rhodes Scholar. He had flown to Montreal, this we knew. He had hitch-hiked to Detroit and there picked up a car to drive for a St. Paul, Minnesota, manufacturing company—this we knew from his telephone call to his sister, Martha, the night before. At 8 o'clock, the dinner growing cold, we had telephoned Decorah, Iowa, and learned that he had stopped to visit his grandmother. He had left there in high spirits. Listening to the 10 o'clock news, Paul's mother made a mental note of the fact that a death on Seventh Street was Minnesota's 405th traffic fatality. No name was given. A few moments later two patrolmen came to our door to ask if we were Paul's parents. The 405th was no longer a number. It was our son.

We are not unlike the other thousands for whom the death toll each year leaps from the pages of newspapers to become a wrenching pain and dull ache. Life goes on, but some of its merriment is gone, never to return.

His brother, Michael, older by fifteen months, had eagerly awaited a few days' talk with Paul before leaving for a three-year doctoral program in theology at the University of Erlangen in Germany. A month later, writing from on board the SS Bremen, he said, "He's in my mind constantly. Paul will be for me what John F. Kennedy says his brother Joe has been for him. . . . Some day I want to see Oxford, but not now."

Grief is as universal as death. Sometimes it may cripple, occasionally it ennobles. The one who grieves may never quite assess its effects. One thing is certain—life is not the same again.

During twenty years as a parish pastor, I had attempted to comfort the grieving. The past six years I had been president of Luther Theological Seminary in St. Paul, where five hundred men were training each year to become ministers. Now the words that had often rather glibly crossed my lips turned in upon me. Could these words carry comfort and peace for me?

Eleven years have gone by since that fateful August night. We have had time to live with grief.

We had prepared to lose him when he was four. A staphylococcus infection of the throat suddenly had blocked off his breathing, and only a quick tracheotomy had saved his life. His mother and I had then reminded ourselves that we would have to try being grateful for the four years instead of being embittered over the added sixty or seventy which he should have had. But we were not ready for August 18.

No one rehearses for sudden and swift grief. One learns after it comes.

Grief is not the occasion for heroism. If we have loved, we suffer. It is as simple and as human as that. Any pretense at bravado or courage is fraud. Whether the tears course unheeding or whether they well up unseen and flow into an aching heart—no matter; to stop them is to distort and twist one's elemental humanity. To grieve is to be human, and to be human is good.

Nor is grief softened by memories. We have the very best. He never gave his parents anything but joy and pride. From the day he began school he won prizes. In a family of six children he naturally shared in the collisions that ought to be there. He worked and frolicked with zest, played football, won his eagle rank in scouting, was elected president of his college's student body, was graduated summa cum laude, and became the school's second Rhodes Scholar. And he was singularly sensitive to the needs of others. But the very excellence of our memories, we discovered, only increased the poignancy of our loss. Memories do not allay grief, at least not at once.

Grief is a lonely role. Hundreds may stand at your side, but deep within you stand alone. Almost immediately letters and telegrams poured in. The first of his Oxford friends to know was Larry Popofsky, a Rhodes Scholar from Iowa and since then a Harvard graduate in law, who wrote, "For us being with Paul was one of the things that made life at Oxford full and rewarding . . . he left his unforgettable image carved in the hearts of those who knew and loved him."

Hands like Larry's were reaching in to lift the load, but the burden was really beyond reach. There are moments when a mother cannot reach a father, nor a brother his sister. Yet there is immeasurable comfort in numbers. A tribal strength surrounds one like a wall. Certainly this is true within the family—and we have four other sons and one daughter, each now married. We close ranks as in a phalanx, but each of us still stands alone.

Grief can easily be embraced and pampered. This I

learned with a shock. I had seen mothers turn from their children yet living to maroon themselves in a continuing, somewhat morbid tryst with the one who was gone. Now this temptation was mine. To leave grief behind seemed wicked, like saying that I had not loved my son after all. Grief became a kind of duty. The only corrective for this mood was to think of Paul himself standing off in the wings or sitting in the bleachers cheering me on to re-enter the common life with zest and verve.

Christmas is the hardest, especially with everyone else accounted for. Following an old custom brought from Norway by my grandparents, we hold hands, circle the tree, and sing Christmas carols. Then the Christmas story is read and prayers said in thanksgiving for the year's blessings before the riotous exchange of gifts breaks loose. Now there are no gifts for him nor from him, nor do we have his Christmas letter. We do not belabor a silence, however. It is easier to speak of him and recall his antics, as if he were still alive. We keep his picture on display. Even his oar is resting against the bookcase, the oar he used in the races of the Henley Regatta in 1960. In the fall of 1961 his mother and I, en route through England, were able one October evening to assemble most of his crew in Oxford. We felt the healing of being surrounded by the young men who had been his dear friends.

Death cannot be made pretty, certainly not for a young man of 24 with the rising plateaus before him. It is not pretty even for a man of 80 when death's slow march has robbed him of the glint in his eye and the spring in his step. In the biblical faith of the Western world, death always has been called an enemy, "the last enemy." God, we believe, is on the side of life, life in all its fullness. Evil and tragedy and death are intruders. In the resurrection of Jesus Christ we have found the clue to death's mystery, and believe that when death has done its worst, God sets his child on his feet again somewhere in his vast empire and puts him to work.

I found comfort in anger. I was not angry with the driver of the vehicle who certainly willed no harm, nor was I angry at God. How could I have God responsible for street accidents, or for the slow march of cancer, or for the bomb at Hiroshima? I could be angry at this "sorry scheme of things entire," where things go awry for both God and man. Some people may be comforted in the thought that God, as a great engineer and architect, arranges everything that happens. I found greater comfort in the thought that God did not want this young life so soon transferred to another part of his enterprises, but that he, too, sorrowed with us and would have wished him to serve now in this world and not yet in some other.

The passing of time does something, but it cannot fill the empty place. Fell a great tree, and a hole yawns against the skyline. No one ever really takes another's place. Every man has a space in existence all his own. Our loss of Paul is indeed well-flanked (nine grandchildren have come since his death). Our other sons do not have their mother's brown eyes and black hair, but they and his sister all reincarnate some of his exuberance and warmth. And we reach out to many of his closest friends as if they, too, through him, have become our sons.

He sleeps in a little windswept graveyard on the prairies of South Dakota, next to his grandfather and grandmother. But he lives on in the fabric of the many lives he cherished and, I believe, ennobled. And with something more than a wistful longing, I believe that he lives and works in another part of the far-flung empire over which the Creator rules. It is in the dimensions of that empire that grief comes tremulously to rest.

Alvin N. Rogness

1. No Time for Dying

You tell me I have an appointment with death. Tell him I have no time for dying. There's too much to live for. You say, all he wants is a moment. I know. Tell him he'll have his moment, but I have no open date on my calendar for him. If and when he comes, I'll let him in—but only for a moment. There's too much to live for on the other side of death, too.

I can't quite understand why death gets such attention when, in the long drama of the years, he gets only one short appearance on the stage—and that at the very end of the play. All the exciting things already have happened by then.

Life, not death, controls the plot. Even if the play is a short one, a month, a year, a decade or two—even then death has but one short act at the end. A month of life can be filled with riches, first of anticipation and then of parents' love and care. And if a person dies at the age of 20, think of how full those years can be—of love, of work, of play, of pleasure, of pain, of sorrow, of joy—the stuff that makes up the story of life, not of death.

When in his "Psalm of Life" the poet Longfellow says,

"Art is long and time is fleeting
And our hearts, though stout and brave,

1

Still, like muffled drums,
Are beating funeral marches to the grave . . ."

he is in fact paying undue credit to death. The years are not funeral marches, but the strident chords of life as it moves from one rich and unpredictable day to the next. All sorts of high aspirations and dreams belong to life, none to death. All kinds of rich memories gather around the events of life, even around the last days of illness, but none around the dull, grim appearance of death.

We live in a strange moment of history. Life presents possibilities never before imagined. The pace of change has become so swift that on the one hand we are terrified, on the other exhilarated, by the unpredictable turn of events that tomorrow may bring. Who knows what the next act in the drama will be?

But isn't this just the stuff of life that makes our days interesting? Tomorrow and tomorrow and tomorrow does not creep in a petty pace, as Shakespeare's Macbeth described life to be. Never has the prospect for a glorious tomorrow for the world been brighter; never has tomorrow loomed up with as many problems to solve. But why are we on earth, if not to help solve problems? If there were no problems, there really would be no reason for remaining here. God honors us by sharing the management of the world with him.

And if we fail, as indeed we will in many instances, he covers our failures. He forgives and forgives, and keeps on giving us new assignments. He does not demand that we succeed. He only asks that we try and try. I like the story of the captain of a Coast Guard rescue crew who ordered his craft out to rescue a ship floundering on the reefs. The first mate protested, "The gale is terrific and the reefs are terribly treacherous. We probably could get out there, but we could never get back." The captain said, "Launch the boat. We don't have to get back. We've got to go out." God has put us on his crew for this kind of commission. He does not demand that we come back; we have no time even to wonder if we will; he asks only that we man the post he has given us. The outcome is his.

I like the last lines of Longfellow's "Psalm of Life":

> *"Let us then be up and doing,*
> *With a heart for any fate,*
> *Still achieving, still pursuing,*
> *Learn to labor and to wait."*

There is much to achieve and much to pursue. Especially is this so if we learn to take time in short spurts, one day at a time. All sorts of little things make up the richness of the drama. A warm greeting to a friend, a piece of work carefully done, an act of kindness to someone in trouble, the support of a worthy cause, a prayer for someone in a hard place—there isn't a day but it surges with countless opportunities to make life rich and meaningful.

There is no time for dying. If we give up, and let the fascinating parade of life go by, all the while waiting for the brief, melancholy appearance of death at the end, we have misunderstood God's plot altogether. God himself has emasculated death, has reduced his part in the play to a quite unimportant incident by dying on a cross and overcoming death in a resurrection on the third day. Because he lives, we, too, shall live. When death's short lines are over, God renews the drama of life on the other side, with

4 APPOINTMENT WITH DEATH

act upon act unfolding in splendor and joy throughout
eternity.

We do not go from life to death; we go from death to
life.

2. There is No Rehearsal

I asked my brother-in-law, a parachutist in World War II, how many times he had to practice (or rehearse) before he actually became a parachutist. He retorted, "In this business there is no rehearsal. The first jump, as the twentieth or the fiftieth, is a do-or-die affair. You make it or you don't."

Death is the one unrehearsed event in a person's existence. There are no practice maneuvers.

On the other hand, from the time a child begins to ask questions until he is an old man, the subject of death is not far from his mind. Every pain is a reminder. The monks of the Trappist Order, pledged to silence, are allowed one greeting to one another, "Remember thou must die." It may be a poor substitute for a cheery "Good morning," but nonetheless it expresses the universal concern of mankind.

Since everyone thinks about death, how much should we talk about it? Should it be a topic for candid discussion with children? Should it be an open subject with people who are about to die?

There is no easy answer. Each situation may dictate what should be done.

A friend of mine, a man in his early sixties, called me to his home one day. He lived alone. His family consisted of one son and a sister. When I arrived he said, "Al, I've just come back from my doctor. He tells me I have six months to live. I'm not afraid to die, but I am afraid to meet God, and you'll have to help me." We spent many long evenings together talking about life, death, God, and eternity. He made me promise not to tell his son or his sister. "Only you, the doctor, and I need to know."

As the disease progressed, both his sister and his son knew. But the three of them never spoke of death. They played out the game of pretense to the end, all three knowing instinctively the thoughts of the others. None wanted to risk the maudlin dramatics which any open discussion would entail. There was no need for words. Love and tenderness found their way in the context of mirth to the end. His house was in order, both materially and spiritually. At my last visit, the day of his death, with his son and sister standing on the other side of the bed he turned to me with a smile and gave me a broad wink. We had played the drama to the end without bungling the lines.

During my twenty years as a parish pastor, I sat at the bedside of many with terminal illnesses. It took me several years before I could broach the subject of death with any sense of ease. It was not until I put myself in the role of the dying one that I finally found it quite natural. I might say, "The statistical probabilities are on my side; I should live longer than you. But who knows. I may not walk out of this hospital alive." Now the two of us could talk as equals. We both had the gift of life; we both faced an inevitable death. Why not talk of both death and life? There is much to be said about each, and they always belong together.

Occasionally it fell to me to talk about the making of a will. There are people who hesitate to make a will for fear that, once the will is drawn, the angel of death would have no further reason to delay his coming. This superstition is more widespread than we would suppose.

It is a sad commentary on man's unwillingness to face the whole spectrum of life, including death, that we find it so difficult to discuss the subject, once death seems near.

We keep running away from both life and death. We settle for questions of secondary importance, even trivial ones. We talk about the weather, how to make money, the next trip we will plan, the sort of man we hope a daughter will marry. All the while we skirt the large question of life itself. What is the meaning of existence, mine or anyone's? What is the overarching goal for man's swift years upon the earth? What of God, and the way God deals with man? It is rare that talk among friends, gathered together for an evening, will go beyond politics, stocks and bonds, food and drink. Yet, deep within each of us is the murmuring of the larger issue—life, death, eternity.

Now and then the great issues surface. And who of us has not experienced the deep satisfaction, even exhilaration, over having shared with friends some thoughts, some longings and yearnings, some convictions concerning life's great meanings?

Even for life, there is no rehearsal. Today is not a preparation for tomorrow. There may be no tomorrow. Each day is a block of time in itself, in which to work, to love, to play, to aspire, to hope. The play is on. There is no time for rehearsal.

3. It's a Bigger Game

Life is more than years, three score and ten—or a few more.

The game is more than nine innings—with possible overtime.

If we are to understand any part of our existence, we shall have to view it in the context of the whole. Like pieces of a jigsaw puzzle, each unit is an exasperating, useless and unmanageable bit until it is fitted into a total pattern.

And if the pattern itself is too small, a fragment of the landscape without the sky and mountains and streams to flank it, why bother with the puzzle at all? If life is no more than birth and death, with some flat, dull moments in between, why ask any questions?

When the hymn writer wrote, "I'm but a stranger here; heaven is my home," he may have been retreating from the surging issues of life. On the other hand, he may only have been expanding its dimensions.

From the dawn of history, every race and people has been haunted, intrigued or exhilarated by the prospect of life after death. Either we must conclude that the intuition of all mankind has been wrong, or we must take seriously this built-in belief of the human race.

If we take it seriously, as I think we ought, then we should try to understand what this intuition means. Why shut ourselves off from the poetry, the legend, the parable, the myth—the faith, if you will—that such an intuition may rightly give? We cannot see the sun after it has dipped below the western horizon, but if its rays are visible to everyone, can we not conclude that the sun still must be there? Is there not a universality about the hope of the after-life which presses the faith upon us?

It has been said that man's hope for an after-life is prompted by his wanting an extension of the life he has known on earth. He hasn't had enough of travel, earning money, making love, eating, playing games, and so on. He wants more of the same thing. So he projects heaven.

This is not true. The desire for an after-life stems from the unnamed longings and yearnings which nothing on earth has quite been able to satisfy. How much like this life the after-life will be is an open question. Biblical faith assures us that there will be no sin, tragedy, pain, sorrow, or death there. In any event the universal desire for an after-life is rooted in something quite different from wanting an extension of this life alone.

We are doomed to want something more than this earthly order can supply. Even when the cup overflows, when our fondest dreams and aspirations are fulfilled, we cry for something more. You have had that experience, and so have I. At the moment of our greatest happiness, there still is a deep melancholy, a reaching out for something more, we know not quite what. The psalmist's words, "deep calls to deep," may express it. We are eternal beings, created for a life with God beyond death, and nothing on earth can fully satisfy us. The days of our years may be three score and ten, but we were created for more than years. We are creatures of eternity.

The longing for eternity is sometimes thought to have emasculated us for this life. If we are promised "pie in the sky when we die," why struggle for pie on this side? If death releases us for something far better, why not invite death? Why bother with the seething issues of this world?

It may well be that faith in the after-life has been distorted to neutralize us for the battles of this life. But this is always a distortion, a miscarriage of the splendid sweep that the eternal dimension can give.

In fact, it is doubtful that man can take seriously the care of this world unless he has been given the dignity and the worth which his citizenship in the next world will give him. The Apostle Paul concluded that if we are no more than earth-bound, with a few, swift years to bother with here, what else is there but to eat, drink, and be merry in whatever grim way we can while the years run out? If, on the other hand, we belong to a life unbounded by birth and death, if we are native to a kingdom which defies death and has but its beginnings on earth, then we have a dignity and a status and a nobility which ennobles every common task on this earth. Justice and mercy, which are the qualities of the eternal kingdom and our basic citizenship, become our prime task on earth.

We are in a bigger game, with bigger stakes and bigger goals. Death is an incident; it is not the end.

4. The Bleachers

They are gone, but they are not gone. They are with God in glory. They have disappeared over the hill, they have rounded the bend, we see them no longer, but they are not annihilated. They have been put on their feet again, to serve God and to enjoy him forever in the more glorious sectors of his kingdom.

Are they now beyond our reach and are we beyond theirs? This haunting question has led men to try all sorts of ways to reestablish communication with those who have died. At unsuspecting moments some people have doubtless been given evidence of nearness, as though we were being watched by our loved ones in the "bleachers."

And who are we to say that the veil that separates the living from the dead may not be a very thin one? Shall we limit God? We sometimes speak of the Church Militant (believers still fighting the battles on earth) and the Church Triumphant (those who have died and now share the full victory of their Lord in heaven) as *one* great Communion of Saints.

In the eleventh chapter of the Book of Hebrews in the New Testament, the writer stages a long parade of people who have lived and died in the Lord, and then in the opening of the twelfth chapter he presents us with this rapturous picture of the bleachers: "Seeing we are surrounded by so great a cloud of witnesses, let us lay aside every weight and the sin which easily besets us, and let us run with patience the race that is set before us. . . ." We are the runners, still on the track; they, having run the race and won, now become the cheering section for us.

We leave ourselves much the poorer if we neglect the support, the pressure and the encouragement of the bleachers.

I found this exhilarating picture of much help in dealing with my grief. The weeks following the death of our son found me embracing grief as a virtual duty. If, indeed, I had loved him, must I not grieve? If I should stop grieving, would this not mean I had not really loved him after all?

It was at this point that the bleachers came to my help. I pictured him among the "great cloud," the sea of indistinguishable faces, cheering me on. I could imagine him shouting, "On with the race, Dad," and when I was able to turn again to the common tasks and away from my grief, I imagined him cheering me with, "Atta boy, Dad, now you're making it." I was honoring him by dropping grief and turning to people and enterprises yet within my reach.

To surrender the bleachers is to leave one with memories only—or with items such as clothing and pictures to hold and cherish. There are people who in their grief have not wanted to remove clothing from closets or trinkets from the table, as if disturbing anything would dishonor the dead. Does not this virtually acknowledge that the loved one has ceased to exist altogether, and that all we have left are these inanimate objects? Is this not almost a kind of idolatry? To be sure, we may cherish pictures, letters, and other tokens which enrich the memories of a treasured past, but not at the expense of a surging present and a rhapsodic future.

A major part of Christendom has in its liturgies kept open the lanes of traffic between the "saints" on this side and the saints on the other. We ask each other in this life to pray for us. When someone dies, this part of the Christian church continues to ask for prayers: "Mary, mother of God, pray for us," and it asks not for Mary's prayers alone, but for those of others now in the bleachers. Other churches, however, have been reluctant to ask for the intercessions of those in heaven for fear that we may finally be praying to *people* and not to God himself.

This caution may be well founded. We are to look to the Lord himself for help. These magnificent "bleacher" lines in Hebrews 12 continue, ". . . looking unto Jesus, the author and finisher of our faith. . . ." The inspiration, the strength, the comfort, and the hope we need for "the race that is set before us" will not come from dwelling on the memories of dear ones in the cheering section. We will need to keep our eye on the Lord himself. However noble and good the person might have been in this life, his life's pattern is not good enough; Jesus himself is the example and model. And whatever inspiration and encouragement may come from "the cloud of witnesses," it is the strength of the Lord himself that must sustain us in the race.

They are gone, but they are not gone. They now belong to the bleachers. Not alone by their memories but by their continuing presence among the "triumphant ones" they cheer us on.

5. Is There Hope?

Hope ought to punctuate every turn in life's road, even the last turn, death. The Apostle Paul said, "If in this life only we have had hope, we are of all men most miserable." Hope is not for the past, nor for the surging present. Hope belongs to a future.

Hope is an exceedingly strong thing. It attaches itself to something that has not come to be. It waits for something. And what a man waits for may govern him more than what he has in his hand. If hope is gone, he really is a rudderless ship. He is at the mercy of the unchanging past and the capricious present. He must have something out there in the future to draw him.

The casualty of our age is hope. The American Dream with its immigrant boundaries ever receding toward the west and with its conviction that on this side of the Atlantic we would at long last create a civilization of justice and plenty—this dream has suffered some telling blows in the last couple of decades. For many people it is all but gone. We are threatened with a paralyzing cynicism concerning the future, whether of America or of the world.

More important than anything else for America and for the world is the recovery of hope. There must be a shining goal which has the power to draw us and to determine our course.

When I think of my children and my grandchildren, I wonder what sort of world they will have by the year 2000. There are times when I capitulate to despair, and wonder whether they will have a world at all. I recoil from these moods to remind myself that I have no right to surrender hope. I look for ways to reassure myself that I must keep an open eye to a possible unparalleled future for them.

I review the staggering changes that have come about in my lifetime. At the time of my birth the Wright brothers were beginning to experiment with airplanes; now we fly the Atlantic in a few hours. There was no radio, no television, no computers, no radar. For thousands of years, from Moses to George Washington, transportation had remained constant. The fastest thing was a horse on a dry track, about thirty-five miles an hour. Within a short century and a half, technology has exploded about us. We fly to the moon.

I cannot regard science and technology as tricks of the devil. I must think of these as gifts from a God who created all these resources and gave to his children the curiosity and skill of mind to ferret them out. He must be pleased with every advance in science, dangerous to our very existence as some of them have become. If man will use these powers with wisdom and justice, the solution of most of our problems—hunger, disease, war—is within reach. The entire world may know an era so golden that, by contrast, other ages will fade into the shadows.

In the face of man's possible misuse of this power and his possible self-destruction, I fall back on my faith that "the earth is the Lord's, and the fullness thereof," that God has not abandoned the planet, that he is still around in a loving

and unpredictable way, and that he is on the side of every
effort a man makes to better this world. I want a hope for
the future, a hope that stretches down the years. I want to
think that every bend of the road may reveal ever richer
vistas, until the day when the Lord himself will return.

What of the hour of death? Is that the end? Is there no
new vista on the other side of this last bend? With the
Christian church of the centuries, I have confessed that "I
believe in the resurrection of the dead and the life of the
world to come." The future has more than a horizontal
dimension, century after century. It has a vertical dimension. There is a hope that soars beyond death.

A woman working as a maid in the home of Ralph
Waldo Emerson had heard a street preacher in downtown
Boston say that the world would come to an end in two
weeks. Frightened almost to terror, she told Emerson what
she had heard, and asked, "What shall we do?" Emerson
replied, "Don't be so distraught. If it becomes necessary, I
think we can get along without this world."

This is the faith and the hope which the Christian faith
has generated all these centuries. Each of us, in his time,
will have to get along without this world. The final turn in
the road is not the final one after all. Beyond death the
vistas only broaden. The goodness and the beauties of life,
tasted here, will be given us in all their fullness there.

6. This Bewildering Century

Are we more preoccupied with death in the last third of the twentieth century than we were in the first third? If we are, what difference does it make for our style of life?

I think we are. Modern medicine has lengthened the life expectancy of all of us. We are better able to outmaneuver the march of disease. But the prospect of some catastrophic, corporate death, virtually unknown during the first third of this century, now hovers over us. World War II and its final punctuation marks at Hiroshima and Nagasaki ushered in a new dimension of anxiety for the world. My doctor and I may be able to avert a heart attack, but what can we do about a possible holocaust?

Never has the world been so jittery. War in Vietnam or the Middle East sends tremors throughout the civilized world. What if they should trigger the unleashing of atomic armaments? We are told that the two dominant world powers have enough missiles stockpiled to assign five thousand pounds of nitroglycerin (TNT) to every man, woman, and child on the earth, not to say anything about more subtle prescriptions for death.

The hope, however feeble, of each of us is that the very possession of such potential for self-destruction will at last shock the world into the awareness that national differences

can never again be settled by war. Slowly we grow to realize
that among nations, as among the fifty states that make up
the United States, differences must be settled by law and
not by violence.

Meanwhile, we live with the peril of wholesale death.

The first decade of this century was one of the most opti-
mistic eras the world has known. Science and technology
boasted one triumph after another; the long day of drudgery for the world was ending. Medicine was lengthening
man's life span. There had been no major wars; Bismarck
had consolidated central Europe without bloodshed. And
Darwin's *Origin of Species,* describing life's evolution from
the simple to the complex, from the primitive to the ad-
vanced, was assumed by philosophers and many theologians
to be the moral and spiritual motif for man himself. A
power within nature itself was driving man ever upward and
onward, from the beast to the angel. Man was essentially
good. Only his primitive environment had made him savage, and technology was changing that. In *The Great Illu-
sion,* published in 1910, Sir Norman Angel pointed out that
the world was now so interlocked, economically and politi-
cally, that in any future war both the victors and the van-
quished would be defeated. And he implied that, knowing
this, man was too intelligent ever again to go to war. It was
an age of optimism.

World War I did not destroy this gallant mood. The
United States entered the war in 1917 with two slogans:
"A war to end all wars," and "A war to save the world for
democracy." On November 11, 1918, the Armistice came,
and we rested on our oars. Utopia was around the corner.
By the end of World War II, no one spoke of the war that
was to have ended all wars. The age of optimism was gone,

the age of crisis was upon us. We now fight a deep mood of pessimism.

Throughout the nineteenth century, we had become so confident of man's ability to solve his own problems, both through natural science and social science, that God had been relegated to an innocuous role, like a venerable chairman of the board who was no longer an executive officer bothering with management. We had lost the centrality of a religious faith.

Now, at this juncture of our history, we suffer a vacuum. Our faith in the inevitable progress of science as the guarantee of a better life is gone. Science threatens, instead, to be the destroyer of both life and environment. Our faith in a God of history is, if not gone, at least an old faith struggling for restoration.

And perhaps restoration is not far off. "In man's extremity, he turns to God." It may be an ungentlemanly thing to do—to run to him in fear. But this may be the first step toward finding him who is less concerned about the survival of the planet than with the restoration of the dignity and worth of man himself.

And the planet is not worth saving if it cannot be the place where man can live with his fellowmen in mutual respect and love. If it is to be no more than an arena in which man slugs it out with other men, whether in wars or in societies of injustice, why should a loving God keep it going? It is in the confidence that it can be more, and that with a new dependence on God and loyalty to him we will make it so—it is in this confidence that we defy the pessimism of the moment and work for a better world.

7. I Want to Die

Quite frankly, there have been times that death has seemed a reasonably welcome escape. I know how the prophet felt when he cried, "It is enough." I've had it!

I am told by psychologists that "the death wish" is not necessarily a symptom of mental disorder. Most everyone has had it, at one time or another. It may not have led to suicide or even to contemplation of suicide. But lurking somewhere in one's mind is that thought that a swift, perhaps heroic, death would solve all the problems.

More than likely, most of our problems are less than tragic. In the economic disaster of 1929—the Wall Street stock market collapse—when men suddenly were reduced from wealth to poverty and committed suicide, one would have to conclude that their goals had been fraudulent to start with. Money should not have become their tyrant. Or when a high school student fails a course, or his girlfriend jilts him and he decides life is not worth living and ends it all, what can you conclude but that he had his priorities mixed up. Neither money nor grades nor a girlfriend should be the whole of life.

Of course, you cannot shrug off many of life's losses. A husband loses a wife whom he has loved for forty years and who has been knit to him in a tight companionship through thick and thin. The death of his wife is almost the same as his own death. They have been one, in a very profound and deep sense. The days ahead look dark and empty. How can he go on? If only he could die.

Death is the only prospect he can entertain with any zest —to die and to be reunited with her in heaven. Deep in his heart, however, he knows that life was not intended to be a happy marriage alone, wonderful as such a gift is. He does not pay tribute to her by wanting to die. Shakespeare's Romeo did not honor either Juliet or romantic love when upon Juliet's death he found life intolerable and ended his own life. If both Romeo and Juliet had had a large enough concept of life, the death of one would not have dictated the death of the other.

How about the person who is dying from cancer? The pain is almost unbearable, day and night. Is there anything wrong with his wanting to die? The doctors have given no hope of recovery. There is nothing left but to await the slow step of death. Does a person have the right to hope that death, already certain, will do its work swiftly and mercifully? He has no option but death. He does not really ask for death. He is no longer allowed to ask for life. He understands the longing expressed in that great hymn, "Come, sweet death."

One of the staggering issues facing us in the future will be the right or wrong of allowing people to die. At this point it may be necessary to define death itself. Is death only the moment the heart stops beating? The heart can be kept beating long after the mind is gone. How arduous should the doctors be in keeping death at bay? Or should they let death come, ceasing all efforts to stop it? If so, who should decide? We may even face the right or wrong of helping death on its way (euthanasia). The assumption in each of these instances will be that death is desirable.

Our modern age has increased the anxiety level of all people and we now have a harder time with hope than a generation ago. What of the future? Fears of all sorts attack us. Unemployment, automation, overpopulation, war—all these are clouds looming on the horizon. Many people, including many young people, cop out. Why try? Why not find escape in some way, in drugs, alcohol, sex—or even death?

In the face of these fears, even the possible death of the planet itself, it is important to engage in the day-by-day tasks of life, and to do so with patience. Three young monks, one of them Ignatius Loyola, the founder of the Jesuit Order, were playing croquet on the monastery lawn. One asked, "If the world were coming to an end in two hours, what would you do?" One said, "I would go to the chapel to pray." The second said, "I would go to be reconciled to my brother." Loyola said, "I would finish the game."

Whatever our fears and hopes, as long as life lasts it is our privilege to carry on.

8. *The Unknown*

We live in a world of cause and effect. There is order in the universe. We have dismissed fairies and gnomes and have substituted for these capricious spirits the precise and terrible computer. We can predict with unerring accuracy. Step by step, with our scientific ingenuity, we have reduced the unknown. Given the known facts of today we are able virtually to eliminate the unknown of tomorrow.

Except what lies beyond death.

There is nothing in the study of man to indicate or prove that the chemistry of his death is any different from the death of the cockroach, the ant, or the mule.

We might say that man alone thinks about death. He is the one rational, reflective creature. But does thinking about death make it less final? Does any amount of thought change the relentless formula, dust to dust, ashes to ashes?

It is only as we leave the neat world of cause and effect, the measurable knowledge of the laboratories, to enter the world of faith that we may have anything to say about life after death. The fact that the belief in life after death is a rather universal intuition of the human race may be some sort of evidence, but it's not conclusive. If we want to journey beyond death, we are forced to change trains. We transfer from the train of reason to the train of faith.

Of course, knowledge about the after-life is not the only unpredictable fact of our human experience. It is not the only unknown. We cannot tell whether the vast power unleashed in atomic energy will blow us off the planet or will make tomorrow's world a much better world. The decision lies with the will of man, and man's will is not altogether predictable. Even on this side of death, the future holds much that is unknown.

But it is death that confronts us with a kind of absolute unknown. If we are to see anything beyond death, we must see with the eyes of faith, and faith is not simply fantasy, a wish-world. To be a man of faith is not to be intellectually naive or stupid. Faith is a most respectable and dignified and useful quality. In fact, without it man's long history would be cruelly impoverished.

The world of faith is built upon a life oriented about God. We make a leap. On the scantest of evidence, sometimes no more than a hunch, we build a whole new world for ourselves. When a person confesses, "I believe in God, the father almighty, maker of heaven and earth," he enters a world which many would describe as sheer fantasy, less solid than *Alice in Wonderland*. It is imagination run wild.

Wild or not, the faith that centers in God has sustained civilization after civilization and has empowered man with more selfless nobility than all the findings of all the laboratories of history. It has given man a dignity and a worth that nothing else has given him. It has made him a prince in a royal house, a citizen in a celestial empire. It has given him a status which defies death. It has enabled him to face the unknown and the unknowables of life with calm and hope.

Every man who has gone through the door (and don't we all in some way or another?) has the feeling that he did not really walk through the door on his own; he was drawn through. Some power greater than his own lured him on. Almost before he knew it, he found himself in the world of faith. In fact, he may have resisted, digging in his intellectual heels to keep from entering, but a mystery greater than man seduced him. He found himself captured by the mystery itself.

There is nothing shameful or anti-intellectual about believing that death is not the end. It is about as natural for man as his desire to eat. But if the belief is to be more than a haunting and tantalizing hope, if it is to be solid enough to live by and die by, God's Holy Spirit must be given a chance to give it substance.

Faith is like that. It waits for the firming up which God alone can do. It is his intention that it become "the substance of things not seen, the assurance of things hoped for." We are asked only that we keep an open mind. We are asked to resist our penchant for doubt and cynicism. We are asked to muster whatever desire and will we may be able to produce. But the creation of faith is God's own miracle. He has put at our disposal the Scriptures and the magnetic figure of Jesus. If we place ourselves within the orbit of his Word and of Jesus Christ, God himself does the rest.

The unknown will still be hidden, shrouded in mystery, but we will live with it as we live with a friend. Faith opens many doors. It opens a door beyond death.

9. A Tantalizing Man

In the faith of the Christian church, Jesus Christ is the clue to almost every question relating either to life or to death. The church has declared that he is God come into view. What we may know about God, and about his dealings with men, center in him. The questions of life and death find light in him.

There is no more tantalizing, magnetic, comforting, or tormenting figure in all the world. He is the one historic character that remains troublesomely contemporaneous. We cannot maroon him in libraries. Genghis Khan, Nero, Alexander, Kant, William the Conqueror, Lincoln, rest quietly on library shelves, awaiting someone's curiosity to meet them. Christ alone roams the world.

We live in a small, shrinking world. Soon we will whisk from New York to Paris in a couple of hours. The fate of Indochina has become the fate of the United States, and who knows what other continents may be at our doorstep? The world cries for wholeness, some end to the fragmentation of national passions and loyalties and the emerging of some world civilization and some world law.

Is there someone who might be the rallying point, some singular person around whom the loyalties and loves of all can focus? Someone who rises above national and ethnic peculiarities, who belongs to all?

There is no other candidate but Jesus, the carpenter from Nazareth who lived two thousand years ago. Mahatma Gandhi, a Hindu, is said to have had but one picture in his room—the picture of Jesus. The churches that have carried Jesus' name have been under attack, and often rightly so. Think of the atrocities that have been either promulgated or encouraged or countenanced by the Christian church throughout the centuries! But never has anyone brought a charge against Jesus himself, the Lord of that church. Pontius Pilate's verdict, "I find no fault in him," is the verdict of the centuries the world over.

This strange aura and power that centers in the lowly carpenter has baffled history. Why should he have such influence after two thousand years? Why should he have been able to find his way through variant cultures and civilizations? What universal quality belongs to him, and what strange power?

It is difficult to answer in any other way than to say that he must not have been speaking nonsense when he said, "All power is given to me, in heaven and in earth . . ." He must be what the early church finally concluded that he was, "God of God, Light of Light, very God of very God." He was, and is, God come to earth. His thirty-three-year life on earth was the one instance when God took on human form and let the children of men see him and hear him.

Moreover, and this is the most important of all, he came on a great mission. He came to suffer, die, and rise again— and in some strange and wonderful way to provide man with the right and the opportunity to live with God again.

The breach that was made long ago is now healed. Man, separated from God by sin and death, now, because of the intervention of God himself in Christ, can rejoin God in a life eternal.

Christ overcame the two gigantic enemies of man: sin and death. He was the victor. However we may define sin —whether as rebellion, disobedience, estrangement, selfishness, madness, meaninglessness—the great message is that in his death and resurrection he settled man's accounts with God. He paid for the sins of the world. He provided forgiveness for sins. Now man, though still given to sin in his day-by-day life, can know that there is forgiveness, and that he can face the future, each day and moment anew, with all the wretched cargo of guilt removed.

He can face his final moment, death, with peace and calm, knowing that the debris of his failures had been taken by another and cleared away. He can face death without dread, its victory fraudulent and momentary. Jesus Christ, the Lord, conquered death by dying and rising, and this dying and rising again is promised to each of his followers, as well.

Death now is but an incident in man's continuing history. Death is not the end of the story for him; it is but a punctuation mark, a comma, in a sentence which stretches on into eternity. It is but the foreword; turn the page and chapter upon chapter unfolds into all eternity.

There is no person in all history who has laid claim to such preeminence and such mission. There is no person today but Jesus Christ who holds such promise for the allegiance of the whole world.

10. Had I Only Known

Remorse is good. Why should we not take inventory of the past? That which we call conscience impels us to do so. It is when our performance of the past is allowed to parade before us that we have some chance to amend, to change.

When a dear one dies, and especially if the death is unexpected, we are faced with remorse of a special kind. Now there is no chance to make things right. The hurts we have inflicted, the vast cargo of indifference and neglect—all loom up to haunt us. We cry, if only I had known that the end would come so soon!

How are we to deal with this kind of remorse?

You can try for a balanced inventory, of course. To be sure, you neglected her often. You said some unkind things. You may have betrayed her. On the other hand, you were often kind. You did love her. You gave her many happy hours. You shielded her from want and danger. On and on —you try to achieve a balance on the good side. But the hurts and the neglects do not go away. You could have done much better, had you only known.

There is no way to handle our shortcomings by listing our virtues. No one can be satisfied with a 51 percent controlling stock on the side of righteousness. The demands of God are for perfection. Even if we could delude ourselves into thinking that we had a nine-to-one balance on the side of goodness, we still would be in trouble. Remorse would fasten itself to the one-tenth.

Suppose a bank teller embezzles a thousand dollars on Monday. During the week he handles, in all, one hundred thousand dollars. When apprehended for embezzlement, he is indignant. He says, "I handled $100,000; $99,000 I handled honestly, only $1,000 dishonestly. And you have the effrontery to call me an embezzler when I have a 99-to-1 balance on the side of honesty."

We are created to be children of God. Like it or not, we are stuck with a conscience which will not let us off with finding extenuating circumstances for our shortcomings. We will never reach peace by balancing off the good qualities against the bad. We are under the law of our Lord who asks that we "love the Lord with all our hearts and minds and strengths and our neighbor as ourselves." And the psalmist utters a profound truth when he says, "There is none good, no not one." It is impossible to push remorse under the rug by listing the good things we have done.

We need to be on guard that we do not feel remorse over circumstances that obviously were not neglects. When our son died, I was tempted to think that the accident could have been averted had I sent him money enough to fly home instead of driving a car. When my father died, I wondered if we had selected the right doctor and the right hospital. Each of us will tend to add to our list of remorse items which should not be there at all.

But there are legitimate items, many of them. I need to deal with them, and I know of no other way than to turn to the forgiveness of God. The list will haunt me until I do. I have no chance to ask my son's or my father's forgiveness.

They are gone. But there is a place of healing, a place where my regrets and remorse can be placed, once and for all.

The Scriptures' remarkable story of God is the key. How does God deal with my sins, my neglects, my shortcomings? He does not overlook them. He does not, in a surge of sympathy, sweep them under the rug. He judges me more completely than any court or society would ever judge me. I stand before his judgment, stripped of every pretense and every defense. Again the psalmist: "If thou shouldst mark iniquities, O Lord, who shall stand?" Any inventory I might have is shattered.

But the God who judges is also the God who forgives and saves—God who, in Jesus, died and rose again to provide forgiveness for sin. He says, "Thy sins will I remember no more." "As far as the east is from the west, so far has he removed our sins from us."

Anyone who has struggled with remorse and has found peace knows this miracle. You may still say, "Had I only known," and wish that you had done things differently, but the anguish of remorse is gone. The forgiveness of God has swallowed it up in a sea of mercy.

11. Why Did She Die?

A child of three dies of leukemia. The anguished mother cries, "Why, oh why, did she have to die?"

Two sets of answers are possible. One out of the world of biology, the other from the world of faith. One does not deny the other. Each has its rightful place.

If the mother asks the doctor, he will give her the biological history of the disease, describing the nature of the illness, its prevalence among children, the efforts to attempt to stop its march, and the final destruction of life. But the mother, satisfied as she may be with this description, cries for some more comprehensive answer—as we all do.

The world of faith has another answer. For two thousand years the Christian world has said some daring and helpful things about death. The mother may ask her pastor, "Why?" He will repeat the story which unfolds in the Scriptures.

"God willed your child to be born. Her coming to you was not simply an accident. She was loaned to you by God for awhile. God, who is on the side of life, wanted only that which is good for her, both on earth and in heaven."

The mother may interrupt: "Why then did he let her die? Did he not want her to enjoy this earth and be useful here?"

"Yes, I believe he did. The Bible seems to say that death was not of God's making. Death is called 'the last enemy,' implying, at least, that God is pitted against death. Death is pictured as an intruder, coming into our world through the back door. Why an almighty God could not have kept it out we are not told, except that he gave the gift of freedom to man—and in some mysterious way the misuse of this gift is given as the occasion for the appearance of death. Don't ask me how this could be. I am comforted with the thought that God is neither the designer nor necessarily in full control of death. I like to think that when your little girl died, God, too, was grieved. He did not want this any more than you wanted it.

"The Bible goes on to promise that when death can do no more, God puts his child on her feet again in another and much better part of his vast kingdom. He is still on the side of life, and death is not the final victor."

When our son was killed in an accident at the age of 24, it was of great comfort to us to believe that God suffered with us, that he had not engineered the accident, and that a life that still could have been so productive on earth was restored in another part of God's empire and put to work again.

There is no demonstrable proof of this, of course, as there is in the world of science, but man needs both answers. The gallant fight against the march of death which medical science has fought these many years is reason enough to take seriously the answers from the world of science. As a man of faith, I would be dismayed and angered if a skilled surgeon neglected the knowledge God had given him, left his scalpel unused and retreated to the chapel for prayer when my child needed his skills immediately in the operating room.

Within this world of mystery, all of us cry for some comprehensive grasp of both life and death. We yield to and embrace the answers that the world of faith can give.

An Anglican bishop from Hong Kong, whom I knew in New Delhi, had lost a son in a motorcycle accident in England. The bishop told me that he had concluded that death had no design, that it struck in caprice. He had concluded that with the "Fall," and the entrance of evil into the world, we were faced with a situation best described as chaos. The ways of God were orderly, but the enemy of God was a being of chaos. There was no point in attempting to find a reason for much of the tragedy, pain, and death that plague the lives of men.

The most important point for any of us who have lost dear ones in what seems a wanton and useless waste of life is that God must not be held responsible. We are not caught in a tight system designed by God. When death strikes its capricious blow, God suffers with us. He helps us pick up the pieces—and ushers our dear one into the glorious dimension of life on the other side.

12. Why Pray?

Everyone prays, at least almost everyone. Driven to the wall, man turns to God. Out of World War II came the phrase, "There are no atheists in foxholes."

Man is basically a dependent being. He cannot keep his heart beating on his own. He has no assurance that his brain will not slip some cogs tomorrow. He cannot indefinitely stay the sure march of death. Intuitively he knows that he is profoundly dependent on something or someone outside of himself. This someone is God.

What of God? I have never seen him or touched him, yet I am the kind of creature who may grow to lean on him more than on anyone or anything else. I learn to talk to him in prayer as naturally as talking to my friend or my mother.

When sickness comes, I summon the doctor. I lean on him and his skills. But behind the doctor and his skills is God. It is he who has given the scientific knowledge to the doctor. It is he who guides the doctor's mind and hand. And when I recover, I thank the doctor—and God.

Nor can I escape the conviction that God can move beyond the skills of the physician. Therefore, when the doctors have given up and have nothing more to offer, I may still call upon God. If the unexpected occurs, and I recover, I may attribute the recovery to the direct intervention of God. Some people call this "faith healing." Whatever it is called, the significant fact is that I set no limits to what God may do. I live by the faith that with him nothing is impossible.

Jesus urges us to pray and pray and pray. He assures us that God will hear. Nor are there limits to the kinds of prayers we may pray. In fact, we are invited to come to him with all our needs, large or small, real or imagined. I want good grades in school; I ask him to help. I want someone to like me, I want to be rid of the pain in my knee, I want a certain job, I want safety on a trip—so I call upon God. I rely on him to sort out the prayers and to give me what is good for me. As a child, in trust, runs to his parents for all sorts of things, we honor God by trusting him for all things. To do less, to come to him only when we are sure the matter is important enough, would be to dishonor him and to grieve him. We are his children.

I have trouble when I pray for something which I am sure is good, and the good does not come. Why does he not answer? Still, I keep leaning on him. There must be some reason for his withholding the grant.

One possible reason is that what I thought was good really was not good at all. He has said, "My thoughts are not your thoughts nor are your ways my ways . . . as the heavens are higher than the earth, so are my thoughts higher than your thoughts and my ways than your ways." It could be that with my limited and sometimes distorted knowledge of what is good and what is not good, I may have asked amiss.

I pray that she might recover. But she dies. I might console myself with the thought that if she had lived, she would have been crippled, demented, or have suffered years of unremitting pain. Under the circumstances, God was good to deny prayer and not let her live.

This is only partial comfort. Why did God let her become ill in the first place, and had she lived, why couldn't he have made sure that her recovery would be complete?

It is at this point that I go to the Bible to learn that in this fallen order, God himself is limited. Why has he chosen to limit himself, or, better still, why did he give the gift of freedom to angels and men and open up the way for disobedience, tragedy, sin, and death to enter? Finding us harried by pain and sorrow and death, why does he stay his hand and allow this state of things to continue? To these profound questions, I find no answer.

The significant thing is that in facing the mystery of evil in our universe, I still keep God on the side of life and goodness. I do strange things in praying to him. I thank him for everything good, and blame him for nothing evil. Inconsistent as this seems, it is the only way I have to have a God who is good. I cannot believe that he wills the death of a lovely little child; I cannot believe that he consents to the genocide of six million Jewish people under Hitler. I cannot believe that he wills the dropping of the bomb on Hiroshima. I must believe that he wills only that which is good.

He has promised ultimately to end this order of tragedy, sin, and death, and to usher his children into a kingdom of unblemished splendor. In the meantime, I lean upon my faith that nothing, that no disaster, will separate me from his love.

13. Why Live?

I ask a doctor, "What do you do?" He replies, "I make people well." "Why should they be well?" "So they can live." "Why should they live?" At this point the doctor cannot draw on his medical knowledge.

I ask an engineer, and he replies, "I build bridges." I ask why. He replies, "So there can be transportation." "Why?" "So people can get goods, clothing, material for shelter." "Why?" "Well, obviously, so they can live." "Why should they live?" No course in the engineering school had dealt with that question.

I ask a farmer. "I raise hogs." "Why?" "So people can eat." "Why should they eat?" "So they can live." "Why should they live?" He might answer, "So they can grow up and raise pigs." But raising pigs is hardly a rationale for all life.

Ultimately we must come to terms with some comprehensive reason for living. We can evade the question altogether, I suppose, and simply go from day to day enjoying or suffering the circumstances that meet us. But like a haunting background melody, the question is there. Why, indeed, should a man live at all?

A rather practical answer might be that we live in order to exact from life more pleasure than pain. If we have garnered 60 percent pleasure and 40 percent pain during our seventy years, we might conclude that life has been good. But this puts us in the class of the looters, who pillage life for whatever happiness they can accumulate.

By exalting such traits as ambition and industry, we unintentionally have given approval to this looting of life. A young man works hard in school to get good grades, in order to graduate with honors, in order to obtain a good job, in order to own a lovely home and belong to the clubs. It is as if he has a bag in his hand and into the bag he gathers his plunder: a good reputation, a lovely wife, a comfortable estate, good health, long life, distinguished children and grandchildren. Upon his death it might very well be said that he did a superb job of pillaging and looting. He outdistanced most of his fellow looters.

However honorable this reason for living might seem in a competitive society, it is not good enough.

Another plausible answer might be, "We live in order to make the world better for our having lived." This is much better. Now we become servants. We set out to give instead of to take.

Praiseworthy as this objective is, it is not strong enough to sustain a man's efforts. He needs to believe that it is possible to make the world better. Looking back over the long march of history, he may conclude that the battle cannot be won. He may decide that in the second half of the twentieth century the world is in worse condition than it was during the first half, despite all the efforts of servant-minded men. Becoming cynical, he lapses into inaction. Why try, when the odds are stacked against you? One might as well eat, drink, and make merry before the final curtain comes down.

When the early church fathers were asked the question,

"Why live?" they came up with what must seem an impractical and irrelevant answer: *"Man should live to glorify God and to serve him and enjoy him forever."*

Nothing in all these centuries can rival this rationale for living. Jesus said, "Seek ye first the kingdom of God and his righteousness, and all these things shall be added," and one might add, "including relevance."

If one sets out to glorify God and to serve him, he is at once plummeted out of the class of the looters. God's interests become his interests. God's enterprises become his enterprises. And God's kingdom operates with justice, mercy, and love—for all men. A man is drawn into the vortex of innumerable causes for the good of men everywhere.

The question of whether his efforts will achieve anything or not becomes only incidental to the efforts themselves. The war is God's war. We need not win it. The outcome is in God's hands. We are asked only to be faithful, to keep on trying and trying and trying, come what may. The planet itself may blow up. The reason for living, therefore, has not been annulled. We never were asked to keep the planet going. We were asked only to do the will of God—to glorify him who gave us life and who, upon death, will renew it in another part of his kingdom.

14. Dignity in Dying

Should a person have the right to choose his own death? Men have done so, from high motives and low. When Patrick Henry said, "Give me liberty or give me death," he was in effect saying that if he had to choose between oppression—the loss of liberty—or death he would choose death. When Socrates refused escape from the unjust sentence of his government and drank the hemlock, he chose his death. When Jesus refused to defend himself against his accusers, he chose death.

Ernest Crosby has a poignant poem on the subject:

> *So he died for his faith;*
> *That's fine, more than most of us do,*
> *But say, can you add to that line*
> *That he lived for it too?*
> *It is easy to die,*
> *Men have died from a wish or a whim,*
> *From bravado or passion or pride;*
> *Was it harder for him?*
> *But to live—*
> *Each day to live forth the truth that he dreamt,*
> *While his friends met his conduct with doubt,*
> *And the world with contempt;*

Was it thus that he plodded ahead,
Never turning aside?
Then let us speak of the life that he lived,
Never mind how he died.

It is one thing to die in the line of struggle for a great cause. It is another thing to choose death as a way out of troubles. We do not think of Socrates or Jesus as suicides. They chose death rather than dishonor, it is true, but they did not cop out. Death for them was a part of a high purpose.

A man left his wife and three children a note saying that he knew they would be better off if he took his life. They never believed him. Whatever his reasoning had been, they thought him wrong. If his burdens were too heavy, if something he had done would bring shame to his family—whatever the reason, they, in love, would rather have had him live. His suicide was, at best, misguided love or heroism.

There are moments in every person's life when the future looks so black that he sees no light through the darkness. A high school girl, for instance, may take stock of her life and conclude that there's nothing left. She's not as pretty as others; no one asks her for dates; her grades are down; her parents badger her; she feels lonely and abandoned. What's left to live for? Besides, the world itself has such colossal problems for her generation to face. She can run away from home, but she has no friends; where will she go? She might try drugs, but drugs cost money and lead only to more darkness. Only one door seems open: suicide. I knew a girl who tried. She swallowed a whole bottle of sleeping pills. Her friends found out in time. After three days in the hospital she regained consciousness. Later she became the wife of a doctor and has a fine, loving family. There were other doors, but the fog was so heavy that she did not see them.

Few suicides involve any clear thinking, and therefore are rarely noble or heroic, even in a misguided sense. Many occur when a person has lost all ability to think. The world does not erect a statue in the park to honor a man because he had the courage to commit suicide. He may have a statue, but it will be to honor him for what he had done in life, despite the last unhappy act.

If a person has cancer, for instance, and faces weeks and months of pain and suffering before what the doctors say is inevitable death, should he not be given the right and dignity of choosing to die? Why wait? Wouldn't his family, too, be spared agony? It's a difficult question. Again and again, however, despite the pain, those weeks of waiting have been for many patients and their families the most tender, loving and memorable moments of a long life.

Deeply etched in the intuition of the human race is the belief that life itself is a great and treasured gift. We tamper with it, either at its beginning or at its end, with trembling caution. The medical profession is trained to fight for life to the bitter end. Their efforts stem not alone from the ethics of science, but reflect the almost universal belief that life is given of God and we dare not deal with it casually.

The underlying reason that life is held in such awe is that man, unlike the white rat or the pig, is created for an eternal life with God. He is not part of a veterinary world. He belongs, as is stated in a rubric of the Christian worship, ". . . with angels and archangels and all the company of heaven." He has a frightening dignity and worth, and it is a universal conviction that man does not exercise this dignity by choosing to end his own life. In our darkest hours, when suicide beckons as the only way, God himself has unexpected doors waiting for us to open.

15. The Options

The reader of this little book will already suspect that the author has a bias. At this point, I ought to be fair and admit that I do. What I write about life and death will certainly not be completely objective. I write from my own experience and from my own faith.

Of course, the subject does not lend itself to objectivity, really. Both life and death have overtones of mystery which even science cannot explain. If we go beyond the boundaries of science, we plunge into the world of fantasy and faith. We are in the world of the poet as well as in the world of the scientist. But perhaps both worlds have their rightful place.

Many of my observations, therefore, will be beyond proof, at least the sort of proof that an age of science normally calls definitive. The great affirmations of the Christian faith, and of any religion for that matter, belong to the world of imagination more than to the world of logical demonstration. I *choose* to embrace them and live by them. Among the many options open to me, I deliberately choose these. They may be true or not true, but deep in my heart I want them to be true, and in a sense, I bet my life on their being true.

There will be many people who, for one reason or another, will choose another option. They will dismiss the great ideas of religion as impractical. They think of religion as a kind of fairy tale. To be realistic, even honest, they think they ought to stand outside the world of religion, and be governed by what they can see and touch, nothing more. When someone dies, he dies. Life is over. "Dust to dust, ashes to ashes," tells the tale.

This may not seem to be an unreasonable option. There is something rugged, something courageous, something honest about going no further. Why not settle for the years that were given? If they were good, fine; if they were not good, too bad. You take life as it comes, day by day, do the best you can with it, and when it's over, it's over. Whatever good memories you can leave are an asset; whatever unpleasant memories are a liability that people will have to forget, if they can. Birth and death are the boundaries.

It is not true that people who have settled for this option are necessarily miserable when the hour of death approaches. Many of them go to their death as gallantly and as calmly as those who have chosen a different point of view. But (and here I reveal my bias) I suspect they are a minority. They may come to terms with their past, be reconciled to those who have been estranged, put their financial house in order, and close the chapter with some degree of peace. But they have robbed themselves of a future. In denying themselves the world of religious faith, they have been impoverished through all their years, not just at the moment of death.

The weight of these short chapters is on the side of faith. I cannot produce proof that one option is true and the other false. I can only hope to lure the reader into electing the one over against the other. If you choose to embrace the world of faith, it will be at some risk. On the other hand, would you not take the same kind of risk in choosing to stay out of this world of faith? We deal with a mystery. It may be intellectually as respectable to choose the one course as the other. To say "It is not so," is beyond proof; to say "It is so," is beyond proof.

I invite you to entertain the prospect for life and death which the world of faith offers you. All you may be able to say is that you want this kind of world. You want it to be true that there is a great and loving God. You want it to be true that he created you to live with him now and forever. You want it to be true that in Jesus he revealed himself and gave you the right to be his child. You want it to be true that God has honored you with a kind of joint management of this planet with him. You want it to be true that he is still around and accompanies you on the way. And you want it to be true that when death is done with you, God installs you in another part of his kingdom to resume a life which has none of the tragedies, pain and sins of this life.

All we can ask of one another is the wistful question, "Do you want it so?" If you do, then you face the mystery of life and death with the kind of posture which will enable God himself to give you a kind of certainty. You may be able to say, with the Apostle Paul, that you *know* whom you have believed or trusted, and this knowing will be something beyond the microscope and telescope. It may be no less real.

16. Dealing with Fear

The opposite of love is not hatred, but fear. Fear turns a person in upon himself and closes the door to any real concern for others. It is when a person's bondage to fear has been broken that he has a chance to love.

Fear has a legitimate place. "We walk in danger all the way," is a refrain from a hymn. A person would have to be stupid or naive not to have fear. Fear is not the opposite of courage. Many a person in perilous moments is almost paralyzed with fear, but fear also can be a catalyst for skill and heroism. It is not true that the only fear we need have is of fear itself. If a tiger is about to leap at you, you had better fear the tiger and not simply your fear of the tiger.

But when fear attaches itself to things you can do nothing about or to things that do not yet exist, then fear is of no help whatever. Most of our fears stem from these sources. The fear of death is one. Death is as inevitable as the next sunrise. To be sure, the sunrise is on a schedule a bit more fixed than your death, but no less certain. The fear of the unknown future is also an instance. Most of us waste more time fearing things that never come to be than things that are here and now. We pull into our craft the unknown cargo of tomorrow, and our frail craft, designed to carry today's burdens, flounders.

The clue to overcoming all illegitimate fears is another kind of death—the death of the self. The New Testament speaks of our dying with Christ. Whatever that means, at least it involves giving up any inordinate concern for our own safety. Had Jesus considered his safety, his first concern, he could easily have outmaneuvered his foes on that first Good Friday. His concern for his own security had died long before he himself died on a cross. He was alive to concerns and values far more important than life—in his case, the salvation of the world. In your case and mine, our concerns and mission are less dramatic, but all of us have the potential for something more important than keeping from dying.

To die to self means that we no longer worry about prestige, power, popularity, or even wealth. Think how mankind suffers because of its need for "saving face." Nations go to war over it. Men become nasty competitors because of it. We dare not do the gracious thing, or even the sensible thing, because of what it may do to our image. We are marooned on the island of self-defense, self-concern, self-pity. Jesus said, "Except a grain of wheat fall into the ground and die it bears no fruit," and "Whosoever loseth his life for my sake shall find it."

The key to death of self is the love of God. It is when a person understands in some little way what God's overwhelming love for him is like that everything else falls into place. Within this love we have no claim on ourselves any more. He alone has total claim to us. He made us, he died for us, he is our companion all the way, he empowers us each moment, he has a life eternal waiting for us. We owe him everything, and he tells us to forget ourselves in the larger task of remembering God and our brother. To the degree that we are able to do this, we also are able to discover the ways of his kingdom. We are set free from the crippling restrictions of self-concern, free to see the wide reaches of God's concerns. Jesus promised, "If the son shall set you free, you shall be free indeed," and added, "Perfect love drives out fear."

A great deal of our nameless fear, the dread that focuses on nothing in particular, stems from guilt. And Christ's death came to grips, head-on, with sin and guilt. He died that the world's sins could be forgiven, swept away, yours and mine. Thus he dealt a deathblow to the basic cause of fear, although we still will have fears.

Tomorrow looms up for twentieth century man with all sorts of anxieties, but they need not be crippling fears. They need not dam the flow of love, day by day. Whatever tomorrow may bring, God will be there. In the meantime, we are given today. And if we are not choked up with fears for our own safety, we are free to turn in love to the surging needs of other people. This will plunge us into the national and international issues of peace and well-being for all men. It will make us sensitive to the cries of people within our own homes and neighborhood.

Even death, our own or that of our planet, will have lost its paralyzing power. We will have died—to self—and have had our lives caught up in the life of God himself. The death of our bodies, or the end of the world itself, cannot stop the onward march of God's eternal kingdom. Fear is gone; we are free for eternity.

17. The Wrath of God

My friend had been given less than a year to live. When he said, "I'm not afraid to die, but I am afraid to meet God, and you've got to help me," he was expressing a deeply hidden fear common to all sensitive men. We all have an intuitive fear of God—unless we have become so calloused to any issue of right and wrong, good or evil, that we have lost our essential humanity.

We cannot shrug off the anger of God against evil and wickedness. If we do, we have a God not worth bothering with. We had better fear his wrath, his indignation. Let us say that God is grieved, even furious, about the sins and wickedness that hurt and destroy his children. Let us say that he is indignant, intolerant, over the breaking of his laws, the very laws designed to protect his children against disaster. If he were less, if he were indulgent or indifferent, could he possibly be a God of love?

This is really the truth of the matter: His wrath is the inverse side of his love. In his book, *The Letters of Luke*, Canon Lloyd has the physician, Luke, say that he was drawn to the little group of Israelites in Antioch because in that large city they were the only people who had the capacity for indignation over the injustice and lasciviousness that ravaged society. Those who were indifferent to evil were finally indifferent to love, also.

In our century there have been two political philosophies of government, National Socialism in Germany and Communism in Russia, that set about to eliminate God, both his wrath and his love. In both, law itself became a casualty. Hitler boasted, "I am the law." In earlier absolute monarchies, the king or the emperor, while claiming totalitarian powers, nonetheless said they exercised those powers "under God." They paid lip-service at least, to a higher law than the capricious passions of man, to the fear of God, whose law and judgment could not be ignored. In the case of both Hitler and Stalin, if they could not have recognized God's love, it would have been a great gain if they at least had stood in awe of God's judgment.

In the Judeo-Christian tradition, God is pictured not primarily as a judge, but as a father. This does not diminish the fact of anger. What father would be worth his salt if he did not punish his children? If he were indifferent to their wrongs which would damage them, if he overlooked the evils in society which threaten to destroy them—could he by the widest stretch of the imagination be regarded as a loving father? I recall an instance when I punished one of my boys. After the spanking he retreated a step, sobbing in anger, and then suddenly he flung himself into my arms, clinging to me, sobbing still. Instinctively he knew that the hand that punished him was also the place of refuge.

We know our heavenly Father is like this—a God of judgment, intolerant of evil, but also a God of infinite mercy, forgiving his children again and again. We know him through Jesus Christ. It is through his dual role as righteous judge and merciful savior that we are allowed to feel his everlasting love.

What can we say about hell, the idea of eternal punishment or everlasting separation from God? We cannot dis-

miss it as an invention of priests to bring people into sub-
jection. And it is difficult to think of a God whose mercy is
far greater than the mercies of men who would levy such
an extreme penalty.

In the profoundest sense, hell is not of God's making.
We who have been given the gift of freedom create our own
hell, both here and hereafter. We choose to have nothing to
do with God and his law, and God fails—he who would
draw us into his kingdom. We have been given the terrify-
ing power to stand him at bay. We can turn him down,
and he has chosen not to force us against our wills. We may
separate ourselves from his love, here and forever. It is not
God who consigns us to hell; this we do ourselves, either
deliberately or by continued neglect.

Even so, there is a longing and yearning, a hope that
God will bring back his straying children, that hell will be
emptied, and that a second chance will be given those who
have turned away from him in this life. This universalism
is given little or no hope in the Scriptures, and we must live
with the sober fact that God's invitation comes to us here
and now. There is judgment, but there also is mercy.

18. Guilt

The feeling of guilt is one of the most common blocks to happiness. Everyone has it. For some it is a dark, heavy cloud hanging over them day and night. For others it is like a melancholy motif of background music, sometimes subdued almost to silence, sometimes swelling to fill the room. Guilt is a dominant problem for the psychiatrist. It is a pervasive theme for writers of fiction and drama. It is a universal symbol of our humanity.

A life that continues to be guilt-ridden is a crippled life. It dampens the joys of an otherwise contented person. It looms up as a major hurdle for the dying. It intrudes into the grief of those who live with memories.

There are several ways of dealing with guilt, some effective and some ineffective, some valid and some fraudulent. One of the fraudulent methods is to deny the existence of right and wrong, of good and evil. Let everything be relative. There is nothing really good, nothing really bad. Good is that which society approves as good; evil is that which society considers bad. Good and evil are nothing more than sociological phenomena. One age and culture may approve, and another may disapprove.

A woman who had been unfaithful to her husband and was deeply troubled came to a friend with her distress. He brushed the incident aside with, "Don't let it disturb you; everybody does it." Why bother your conscience with it when the culture of our day takes it for granted? If she had been able to deal with her guilt in this way (she wasn't), she would not have seriously considered right and wrong. She would have surrendered her basic humanity.

A second fraudulent and ineffective way is to blame others. We blame heredity and environment. How can I be any different? My grandfather had an uncontrollable temper, too. Or, how can you expect me to behave differently when you consider the kind of people I work with? Moreover, my father and mother never gave me love. My twisted nature is the obvious result of a combination of hereditary pressures on the one hand and environmental pressures on the other.

To deal with responsibility and guilt in this manner is to deny that man has any freedom of choice. We are caught in the relentless wheels of life and are no more than cogs in the irreversible machine. We are driven by biochemical forces, by appetites and desires, by inclination and disposition, and have nothing to say about what we are or what we do. There is a determinism, a fatalism, and ultimately a nihilism which make any pretense at responsibility (and therefore guilt) utterly false.

Unhappily, neither of these methods will work, for the simple reason that there is such a thing as good and evil in the universe, and for the further reason that man is created with the gift of choice. He cannot settle for "everybody is doing it," and he cannot really pass the buck. He is doomed to deny both methods. He knows there is right and wrong, and deep down he knows he is a responsible being.

Forgiveness—forgiveness of sin—is the only answer for guilt. There is no other. But how is a man to be forgiven for all the hurts that he has done and for all the good he might have done and failed to do? Can he retreat into the past, search out the people he has injured in one way or another, and ask their forgiveness? How far-reaching will be his search, if he is really to find all the people he has hurt? Especially does this become an endless hunt if he is to ferret out all who have been neglected and overlooked. And Jesus pointed out that is precisely what is asked of us—to find the hungry whom we did not feed (but might have), the sick we might have helped (but did not), the discouraged we might have strengthened (but did not).

Moreover, if we could find them, would they forgive us? The hurts may be too deep and reconciliation impossible. The wounds may still fester. Hostilities and bitterness may go on unhealed. We must try, but we may fail.

It is at this point that faith comes to the rescue. At the very center of life with God there is forgiveness. Your father whom you hurt may be dead, your brother may be beyond reach, your wife may be unable or unwilling to forgive. But with the Lord there is forgiveness. Your sins, many as they are, are taken away. "Your sins will I remember no more," is his promise. You stand without guilt, as if you had never sinned. There is no greater miracle of healing in all the world.

19. What About Heaven?

When someone says, "This is heavenly," he doubtless means that something comes close to meeting the heart's deepest longings and joys. When a congregation sings, "Therefore with angels and archangels and all the company of heaven we laud . . . ," they are expressing the ecstatic prospect of a fulfillment which cannot be achieved this side of death.

On the other hand, the hymn ". . . earth is a desert drear, heaven is my home," does not really express any universal verdict. Earth is not a desert drear for most of us. We find much to live for. The beauties of nature, the love and friendship of family and friends, the tingling of good health —these are the great, good gifts of God to his children on earth. We need not wait for heaven. The earth, too, belongs to the Lord, and his blessings are rich and varied here also.

But there is tragedy, sin, pain, injustice, and death—on this side. On the other side they are gone forever. Whatever else we may say about what heaven is, the Bible is clear about what heaven is not. Unhappiness and sorrow are replaced by joy.

When we set out to speak about what heaven *is*, we are driven to pictures. It is a home where we live with God and our loved ones forever. It is a place of unparalleled splendor, streets of gold and gates of pearl (or whatever else of beauty and grace may appeal to the imagination). It is a place of rest, it is a place of work, of service. There is the suggestion of rapturous music. Most of all it is the place where God lives, and we shall live there with him.

Any picture we use belongs, of course, to our own world of time and space. It is impossible for us to find images outside of our own experience. If we are to believe in an after-life at all, perhaps there is nothing wrong in letting our imagination play rather freely with the imagery the Bible provides.

First, exclude everything bad and include everything good. Few people would want a heaven which was but a repetition of the woes of this life. Nor are we, on the other hand, anxious to exclude from heaven the good things in this life. Why limit our concept of heaven or of God to vague and fragile qualities? When a little boy asks if his puppy, killed by a car, will be in heaven, is there anything wrong, even biblically, in replying, "Perhaps he will; who knows?"

After reading C. S. Lewis's fantasy, *The Great Divorce*, it occurred to me that I had pictured the people in heaven as "wisps of vapor" floating about, nodding to one another in a kind of non-corporeal, ethereal, misty or spiritual world —over against the hard, solid stuff of this world—when all the while I should have been reversing the picture. Heaven is the more real, and therefore the more lasting. These earthly bodies of ours are the impermanent ones, with cells dying and being replaced by other dying cells until death wins the certain and final round. The spiritual bodies, the glorified bodies which Scripture promises that we shall have, are the permanent bodies.

It may be naive to let one's imagination run a bit riot, but it is not naive nor is it unbiblical to find ways to affirm that heaven is a full life in a permanent home with God.

The more poignant question is whether we shall know one another there, and whether the affection we have had for one another can be restored and continued there. To this question the Bible seems to give an unequivocal yes. Our love for one another will assuredly not be less. It may be somewhat different, but the difference will only enhance what we have known of love. A boy of five, observing his sister and her lover, may conclude that love is primarily candy and flowers (which he brings her). Only later will he understand that candy and flowers were but symbols, and secondary ones at that, and that love was much more. Heaven may introduce us to new and more splendid dimensions of love than we ever knew here.

When I asked a boy of 17 if he had given much thought to what heaven would be like, he replied, "No, I'm more interested in what life on earth can be like. I'm satisfied to leave the makeup of heaven to God. It is enough that I will be with him." I liked his answer. Reunion with our dear ones is, of course, one of the treasured dividends, but it is the presence of the Lord that crowns all of heaven's gifts. I belong to him, and it is he who has given me life and who loves me; to be with him forever is heaven.

20. Memories

Our Lord evidently wanted us to concentrate on the present, and not be lost either in memories of the past or in fantasies of the future. "Be ye not anxious for tomorrow," he said, and "When you pray . . . say, Give us this day our daily bread," and further, "Leave the dead to bury their own dead."

But the present cannot be divorced from the recollections of the past or from the hopes for the future. Life is one piece. Like a river, any segment is a flowing part of the whole.

Those who grieve over the death of a dear one often have problems with memories. They may go to either extreme. They may be so absorbed in memories that the present becomes virtually meaningless. They may deliberately block out memories, in self-defense, and rob themselves of riches which should be theirs.

Death does strange things. During the two years when our son was in England studying, he was often in our minds, of course, but not more so than our other five children. Upon his death he seemed to be constantly in our minds. He haunted us. Night and day there was hardly a moment, when immediate pressures did not demand attention, but that memories of him did not surge into view. In retrospect, I don't see how it could have been any different.

There came a time, however, when we had to choose. Would we actually cultivate this somewhat eerie presence? Would we deliberately blot out his memories? Would we talk about him on every possible occasion, or would we never mention him?

It helped to think that he was not really gone. He had been on the other side of the Atlantic; now he was on the other side of death. But he lived. His life was not extinguished, like the flame of a candle. The Lord had given him a resurrection. He belonged to the great company on the other side. The continuity of life which he had with us and which death had severed had been restored. We could not write to him or he to us. But even on earth we had not been dependent on letters or on seeing him. Our lives were tied together, explicit communication or not. They still are.

By not letting death be a morbid end, we achieved a proper place for our memories. They give us both pain and joy, mostly joy. Whenever the family is together, we move in and out of conversations about him almost as naturally as we do about the children still living. "That's just like Paul." "Remember how he would always forget where his billfold or cuff links were?" We are drawn to Sidney Poitier's movies because he has so many of Paul's mannerisms.

Memories are too important, too rich to exclude from life. The capacity to remember is a great gift from God. Past, present, and future belong together. Someone has pointed out that time is so swift and short for a man of 60 compared with a boy of 10, because a year for the boy is one-tenth of his existence and for the man but one-sixtieth. The year is always in the context of the number of years, and memories are woven into the warp and woof of the fabric of the whole.

But what do we do with the unpleasant memories, those that hurt? One thing is certain: to exclude memory altogether in order to escape the unpleasant ones is the wrong thing to do. Simply to sort out the memories, subdue those that are unpleasant and let the good ones surface, probably will not be possible. Something more is required.

The key to have the hurtful memories disappear is the forgiveness of God. I know of no other way. If I have wronged him who is gone, there is no way for me to make restitution. If he has wronged me, there is no way for him to reach across the chasm of death and assure me that it's all forgotten. Both of us need someone who in an overarching forgiveness can eliminate the sins and guilts for both of us. This is what the forgiveness of God does. It is forgiveness for both of us. "Thy sins will I remember no more," is the promise he gives to each of us, and we, separated by death, have the right and duty to join the Lord in forgetting. He who is with the Lord has risen above all sin and guilt. I who remain have a duty and right to be forgiven and to have all unpleasant memories forgotten.

It takes God to do this. No amount of reflection or rationalization on my part will do it. Try as I will to push guilt and remorse away, they continue to push their cruel way into my memories—until I have deposited them with God and let them rest there. Then I am free to dwell on the good memories, to regale my friends with incidents from the past, to cherish the good hours that we had together, to anticipate the joy of reunion.

21. The Forgiveness of God

I could not stand God if he were not a forgiving God. The glory of the Christian faith is that it centers in the message of forgiveness.

At first sight, a religion of forgiveness might seem too easy. Can there really be forgiveness for men like Nero or Hitler or Stalin—or for men like me? Can God really overlook the crimes, great or small, which human beings commit?

He does not overlook them. God is a severe judge. He sees the inner workings of a man, his desires, his thoughts and motives. A man may control his behavior in such a way that the world gives him a verdict of praise and upon his death a splendid obituary. Before God's high court it is different; the exacting law of God condemns him. "If thou, O Lord, should count iniquities, O Lord, who shall stand?" says the psalmist. "I am undone," cried Isaiah.

It would be cruel to usher a man before this high, eternal tribunal if the only possible verdict would be judgment. The psalmist goes on, ". . . but there is mercy with thee . . ."

Forgiveness plunges us into the very heart of the Bible's picture of God. Throughout the history of Israel in the Old Testament we have the recurring theme of God forgiving a rebellious and stubborn people. In the New Testament the theme comes to a climax in the story of Jesus.

One of the pictures painted by the New Testament is that of a courtroom, with Christ as the judge of all, in heaven and on earth and man appearing before him for judgment. The court has but one possible verdict: guilty. Then a strange thing happens. The judge steps down from his bench, and takes the sentence himself. In a sense, he exchanges places with man. He goes to his death for man. He assumes the guilt of man, and transfers the innocence of God to man. In the language of the theology of the church, he imputes (or attributes) the righteousness of God to man. Now man stands bewildered in the court. Suddenly he is innocent and the Lord is guilty. Man is acquitted and God is sentenced.

This may be a cold and inhuman picture. After all, God is more than a judge; he is a Father. Jesus is more than a legal figure; he is a Friend and Brother. The relationship between God and man is more than a juridical one. It is a warm, family relationship. We are his children, after all, and not criminals at the bar of justice.

But the image is nonetheless a profound one. It recognizes a deep difference between good and evil in the universe. It takes seriously the fact of man's shortcomings and sins. It takes seriously that judgment is demanded, that we cannot brush aside the stark fact of right and wrong. It puts into bold relief the mercy of God.

Moreover, it makes Jesus' death more than an example of a man dying heroically for his convictions. It becomes, instead, the sentence of the universe upon sin and evil, the payment for the sins of the world and for my sins. However difficult it is for us to understand this, the truth is that God himself has suffered and died *for us*. He has taken neither sin nor mercy lightly. A forgiving God has paid the supreme price for being this kind of God.

The Christian church never would have survived the first century if Jesus had done no more in his life, death, and resurrection than demonstrated to man how a noble life could be lived. We have seen all sorts of heroic people do that: Socrates, Paul, Joan of Arc. Instead, millions of people these many centuries have believed that Jesus brought forgiveness of sins to the world. Man, now the forgiven one, attained, through Jesus' death, the right to be restored to the Father and to live with him, sinless, forevermore.

If any man will take his wrongs, or sins, seriously, and if he understands in some little way what guilt really means, then a forgiving God becomes the most powerful force for good that he knows. A God of judgment, whose only concern was to pressure man to perform better and better, and who finally would reluctantly accept him on the basis of his choppy record, would not generate any special gratitude in man. Only a merciful God, a God of grace, who accepts man because he loves him—only this sort of God can move man to the kind of thanksgiving which will make him want to do the will of God.

God has risked everything, not on badgering man with judgment, but on winning him and luring him with love.

22. The Art of Comfort

How as a friend will you comfort someone in grief? Most of us are bunglers. We may even be afraid to try. We stand off to the side. Our words, if we offer them, seem clumsy and empty.

Our Lord told us to "bear one another's burdens." This is relatively simple if a man is short of money and you write him a check, or if he is hungry and you give him a meal, or if he is suffering from injustice and you throw yourself into efforts to achieve justice for him. Whenever there is a need and a way to meet the need, the problem is simply one of will. Are you willing to try?

It is not always as easy with other sorts of tragedy, including death. How do you help someone whose whole world seems to have dropped out from under him, and who is on the brink of despair? If you are "to weep with those who weep," how do you go about it?

One simple and effective way is to be at their side. Quite apart from anything you say, your presence is a language of sorrow and love. And it may be the most eloquent language for the moment. The Bible says that when Job's comforters came to him in his hour of overwhelming loss and pain, they sat with him for seven days and seven nights without saying a word, "because they

66

saw that his grief was great." This was the kindest thing they did, for when they broke silence and began to talk, their conversation was far from comforting.

Many a person, well-meaning, has used words at the wrong time, words which though pious and "religious" were little more than empty phrases and were proof that the person was insensitive to the dimensions of grief. Great sorrow plunges the grieving one into a state of shock, and words have no cohesion. Communication must be beyond words—a presence, a tear, an embrace—in silence.

I shall never forget the moment, the day after our son's death, when two of my dearest friends came, one from across the continent. I saw them through the window, coming toward the house. A dozen sermons on death would not have been as eloquent. Another friend, an eminent theologian, wrote a simple note of affection and said that the great words from God would at the moment probably carry no freight, but the time would come when they would become carriers of comfort again. They have.

To be surrounded by people who care is great comfort. Burial and funeral customs vary from nation to nation, culture to culture. In most instances, however, they involve a community. People gather. In our earlier immigrant days, everything stopped, even in the midst of harvest. Even in our earlier urban society, stores and shops would close and everyone would come, whether they knew the dead well or not. The death of one was a community loss. Some people also would come simply as a tribute to death itself, this stark reminder of life's impermanence.

Our highly complex and urban life has made these customs almost obsolete. Unable or unwilling to take a couple of hours off for the service, people will trickle through a funeral parlor the night before, pay a brief visit to the grieving, write their names in a book, and go on their way. At the service itself, the grieving family may be marooned safely in some nook, away from the view of others present. Well-intentioned as these practices may be, they rob the grieving family and the community itself of the opportunity to *be one* in grief.

Coming back to words. The great promises of God in Scripture are, of course, channels of comfort. Especially is this true if people have heard them since childhood, have spoken them or sung them as a part of the liturgies of the church and, therefore, have them deeply etched in their minds and hearts. The words will carry freight, because they are God's own way of reaching in.

Any wrenching grief is a lonely experience. Joined as they are in a common loss, children who have lost a father or mother nonetheless suffer alone. Or a father and mother in the loss of a child, however deeply they love one another and now share a common grief, cannot reach in to the deepest recesses of the heart to lift one another's pain. Great grief drives one to a lonely island.

It takes the miracle of God's own comfort to reach the depths. After all, we belong to one another for a day. We belong to God for eternity. He made us, he holds us, and he has destined us for an everlasting life with him. We come from God, we return to God. This is man's shortest and most comprehensive biography. It is in the very nature of our being, therefore, that from God, his presence and his promises, peace and healing must come.

23. Life is More

Life is more than an accumulation of years. Its measure is essentially qualitative, not quantitative. Once we understand this, we may be less anxious about stretching out the years. Whether we live five, twenty, or eighty years, the measure of our worth must be by a different standard than the interval between birth and death.

The apparent tragedy of an early death will be seen in its proper perspective if we have clearly in mind what constitutes a meaningful life.

In our industrial society, it is commonly accepted that a man's importance is measured in terms of his production. And production itself is a bit elusive. The man who his whole life through stands on an assembly line, an indispensable link in the production of automobiles, is thought to be less productive than the sales manager who, producing nothing concrete, nonetheless earns five times the salary of his brother on the assembly line. Money becomes the measure, however fraudulent.

Whether an automotive worker, a farmer, a builder of bridges, a man has dignity and worth which is measured by some standard quite apart from production. Man is important because God made him important. He is somebody, not because he has been a successful competitor in

production and has become wealthy or powerful. His
dignity, his worth, derive from quite another quarter.

Nor does it come from nobility of character, vastly more
significant though this might be. To become a man of
justice and mercy, whose efforts are poured into making
the world a better place to live, is indeed the more
laudable standard. Even by this standard, how can we
assess the importance of a child whose life is cut short by
an accident at the age of four?

The exhilarating perspective God has given us is simply
that at creation (or at birth) he endows a life with
dignity and worth. Whether the child is retarded or grows
up to be a brilliant scientist or philanthropist, his worth is
assured. He is a prince in a royal house. Nothing can
change that, years of achievement notwithstanding.

It was gratifying for us to receive a large number of
letters following our son's death—letters that spoke of
kindnesses which he had shown others. But our son was
not yet in the channels of production. He had completed
his work in the "modern greats" at Oxford, and was looking forward to further education, either in law or theology.
He might have died at four, when for a few hours we
thought we had lost him. An emergency tracheotomy
saved his life. But whether at four or at 24, the measure
of his importance could not have been in terms of production. He was a somebody because God had made him a
somebody.

It is difficult to embrace this criterion of a man's worth
without also embracing the sweep of life which does not
end at death. If a child dies at three, is that the end? No,
the life which God has designed for us, and to which
he has assigned such dignity and worth, must presuppose
a dimension which the years, short or long, cannot limit.

To be sure, a mother and father may say of a child (dying at three, for instance) that even these short years had brought untold blessing to them and to brothers and sisters. But for a genuine overview of life, this is not enough. They will cry for a larger answer. They will yearn for an eternity. They will want the death of their child to be but a door through which he finds a fulfillment which not even eighty years here could have given.

For nearly twenty centuries millions of people have been sustained in the faith that because Christ rose from the dead, we, too, shall rise. His death and resurrection are the guarantee that God loves us and the assurance that the power of death is broken. Because he lives, we, too, shall live.

Nothing in history can compare with the power for courage and hope that this faith has given us. The life of a common carpenter in a corner of the world centuries ago has baffled the world, but has sustained it, too, and it continues to do so still.

24. The Pilgrim

The last part of the journey should be the best, at least
for the pilgrim. He has wandered through a country,
perhaps somewhat foreign, on his way home. I once
asked a friend of mine, now 81, how his retirement years
had been. "They have been the best of all," he replied.
"The last years of a man's life are the best."

If a man can say that with charity and mellowness, he
most likely has thought of the whole of life as leading to
a goal, a fulfillment.

One of the most colorful men I have known through
the years was Bishop Eivind Berggrav of Norway, whose
rich and turbulent life led him through the resistance
years of the Nazi occupation and who became a leading
figure in the World Council of Churches. I love this letter
which he sent to his first little parish just before his
death:

"We are getting old, many of us now. I was 74 this
fall, . . . But every Christmas I feel somehow younger,
almost like a child. The difference comes from the fact that
eternity is so much closer now. The busy-ness is over,
the quiet is growing. The last Christmases I have spent
at Oivind's [his son], where there are five children and
much Christmas! At times I think that my father and

mother and especially Kathrine [his wife] are there to rejoice with us. . . . And so I am sitting in my deep chair, not knowing whether this is my last Christmas. There is nothing sad about the thought. An old man with a life full of weeds and wounds—unbelievable as it sounds—has had imputed to him, by God, that which his Redeemer has done for him, and is graciously accepted as a child of God." *

He had faced death many times, both in the risks of the war resistance and later with his recurring heart attacks. He had led a full and rich life, achieving much. His calm came, however, not from a review of his triumphs, but from a life that had been a journey toward an end and a fulfillment assured him through by his Lord.

It is a superb gift of the spirit to entertain the end of life as the most exciting and the most desired chapter of all. This cannot be done if our chief end in life is to pit ourselves against the deterioration of the body. It cannot be done if our dominant concern is the survival of the planet. We must calmly accept the fact that both the body and the world inevitably will end.

There is nothing wrong with wanting to live long. Life is a gift, and we ought to take reasonable precautions to keep it, but not at the expense of living well or nobly. We journey, not merely to be on the move. We have tasks to do on the way. If the doing of the tasks shortens the journey (our years), so what? A doctor cannot refuse a cry for emergency help because he needs eight hours of sleep to lengthen his life. A football player cannot refuse to carry the ball for fear that he might get hurt. You

* Alex Johnson, *Eivind Berggrav, God's Man of Suspense.* Kjell Jordheim, tr., with Harriet L. Overholt. Minneapolis: Augsburg Publishing House, 1960, pages 219–220.

cannot put the body first, either its safety or its long life. When Patrick Henry said, "Give me liberty or give me death," he knew that there were things more important than dying at 90.

Our age is almost neurotically preoccupied with health. We chatter about diets, periodic health checks, early retirements, as if the meaning of life is essentially the length of life. Instead, we need some great meaning for life. We fail to embrace death as a "coming home," a kind and gracious end which opens a door to unpredictable possibilities for significant life and service on the other side.

For want of some comprehensive purpose in life, our retirement years become an almost intolerable burden. Our day-by-day reason for carrying on was the job, a sort of fragmentary, piecemeal necessity for keeping the body fed and clothed. Now the job is gone. The body begins to creak at the joints and the step grows slow. What is there left but to brace up this body-house the best we can, and wait in melancholy for its collapse? We might distract ourselves with trips, endless nights and days before television, and other escapes, but what is that for someone who was created in the image of God, who was given a world and his brothers to care for, and who has the rhythm of eternity in his spirit?

"Love God with all your heart . . . and your brother as yourself," is the clue which Jesus gave us for the pilgrimage, and then went on to assure us, "I go to prepare a place for you."

25. ... With Thanksgiving

I can't be thankful that our son was killed at 24; I can be thankful that his 24 years were filled with zest and love.

The Apostle Paul tells us ". . . in nothing be anxious but in everything . . . *with thanksgiving* . . . let your requests be known unto the Lord," and also, "All things work together for good to them that love the Lord." We are not naive enough to believe that we have reason to be thankful for everything, or that everything that happens is good.

But in the midst of evil and tragedy there is goodness and there are blessings. Life is a mixture of both, and it is far better to concentrate on the good things with gratitude than to dwell on the disappointments with bitterness. Moreover, it is important to believe that God never engineers that which is evil.

I cannot be thankful that countless thousands of Americans and Vietnamese lose their lives in what seems a meaningless war, or that millions within our own country suffer injustice, hunger, and despair, or that a major part of our national effort goes into armaments. I can find all sorts of reasons to be bitter.

But I need not be blind to the tragedies of life in finding reasons, also, to be thankful. And this I know for sure, I would much rather go fishing with a man whose spirit is filled with thanksgiving than with a man whose spirit is sour with bitterness. If I want to be of any value to my friends or to society as a whole, I must be on the side of gratitude.

I start with God, who created me and gave me life, who loves me, who died for me, who is my companion, who picks me up when I fail, who suffers when I suffer, who is always on the side of life, and who, when death can do no more, puts me on my feet again in his own imperishable kingdom.

Long ago I ran across a little poem entitled "The Atheist's Wail." I have forgotten the precise lines and I am unable to find the verse again, but the poem said, in effect, "I can stand to writhe on a bed of pain and not need God; I can stand at the open grave of a loved one and steel myself and not need God. But when the autumn trees are in full color, and I'm walking through the woods with my beloved's hand in mine, it's a terrible thing not to have anyone to thank." We all need a God—to thank!

It is doubtful that any one of us can sustain a spirit of thankfulness, through the ups and downs of life, without a faith in this kind of God. There are "religious people" who misunderstand God altogether, who regard him chiefly as a law-giver, who never have grasped the reaches of his mercy, and who themselves find very little in life to generate gratitude. They are dour, they are harsh in their judgments, their sense of humor is gone, and they are strangers to joy. They may be Christians, but they have missed God's great gifts of graciousness, mirth, and gratitude.

Much is written today about the disenchantment of our youth. We give them a world made wretched by two gigantic wars in this century and a weary decade of deaths in Indochina. We put into their hands the triumphs of technology which threaten the life of the planet itself. We plunge along with the gross national product still the boasted measure of our greatness as a nation. And we wonder why it is difficult for them to be the grateful beneficiaries of our legacy.

But they, too, if they are to manage this world, as they shortly will, for themselves and for their children will need to overcome cynicism and bitterness which will only paralyze them for the gallant action which can be theirs. They are the hope of the world. If they can, despite all the critical issues to be faced, believe that the God who made the universe is on their side in righting the wrongs of the past, and if they can be grateful that they have him at their side as a mighty ally, then they may avoid the panic and disenchantment which could immobilize them—and lead the world into a new and glorious era. It will take more than faith in us, their elders, however much we may be on their side. It will take more than faith in the past. It will take a faith in God.

"Thanks be to God who giveth us the victory, through our Lord, Jesus Christ," is the bold affirmation of Paul the Apostle. What victory? It was a grim world. Roman dictatorship encircled the Mediterranean. The small Christian group was persecuted in almost every land. There was no blazing prospect of a world Utopia. Still Paul cried, "Thanks be to God who gives us the victory." Obviously the victory was more than the survival of the planet. It was, and is, a life with God here and hereafter which death itself cannot destroy. This is the key, the center, of continuous thanksgiving.

26. Grace

Our universe is so vast that any attempt to bring it within our imaginations leaves us breathless. The quasars, we are told, are huge bodies, a billion times larger than our sun, and seven billion light years (the distance we could travel in one year at 186,000 miles per second) from the earth.

Facing on the one hand the mystery of this incredibly large universe and on the other hand the claim that God, who made it all, bothers with me on this tiny speck called earth—how can I do anything but throw up my hands in despair?

Against this possible despair, I have the audacity to believe that God does bother. I may even entertain the staggering thought that I am more important to God than any quasar. What he succeeds in doing with me is more critical than how he manages these wheeling suns and planets.

Unless we give up any thought about the mystery of the universe, of life and death, and settle for the daily round of eating and drinking and reproducing our species, we must make some bold and presumptuous claims about God. If God does not bother with me, why should I bother with him? If I can't bring him into my bedroom when I pray, I might as well leave him out there in the galaxies somewhere.

God does bother with me. How he deals with me is best

described in the Christian concept of *grace*. He is not a celestial machinist who makes me a cog in some relentless machine. He is not primarily a judge or policeman who hedges me in with rewards and punishments. He is a father, and I am his son. He has made me to be like him, with freedom to obey him or disobey him, to love him or to ignore him. He wants my love. He has staked everything on winning my love. Failing this, he has lost everything with me. And his strategy for winning me is described by the term, "the grace of God."

In a profound sense, God sets out to give me everything and to demand nothing. All he wants is *me*. He cannot have me as a cowering, reluctant prisoner. He has no place for prisoners in his kingdom. There is room only for those who have come to him willingly and gladly in love. He cannot, therefore, send a heavenly police force to badger me into his house. Instead, he sent his only Son, and he sends his Holy Spirit to help me see how much he loves me and wants me.

If I remain untouched by this, if God is only someone to fear or ignore, not to love and to thank, then God has lost me. His grace did not reach me. His lavish, unconditional love left me cold. I am his son, to be sure, because he created and redeemed me, but I am beyond his reach—a lost son, a dead son, a son still floundering away from home in the far country. And God has no new way to reach me. If he cannot reach me with the spectacle of his own great love for me, he can do nothing but grieve over the loss of a son.

The secret of grace is that God does not ask that I look like a son, behave like a son, or even think like a son. He only asks that I accept him as a father and come home. And when I come home, he does not taunt me with my failures or test me to see whether I can stay as a son. He only *asks* that I stay. In staying, it is quite likely that the contagion of God's way of life will do something to me. I will change. But I do not change in order to be or become a son. I am his son by grace alone. My sins are forgiven. My right to sonship has been guaranteed me through Christ. This is the miracle of the kingdom. This is the key to understanding the dimensions of the love of God, the key which has opened the doors to the Father's house.

It is not strange that we have a hard time believing this. Who wouldn't? Isn't it, after all, a sort of presumptuous madness on the part of a human being on this small speck in the universe to believe that the great God can love like this? And can trouble himself with the three billion people on this earth, one by one?

But what is the alternative? If I do not believe that God cares, that he has time only for keeping these wheeling planets and suns from colliding, then I am left on my own with no comfort but with waning courage. I have no answer for the great questions of life and death.

And so I choose to rest in the love of a God who wants me as a son, who has gone to unbelievable lengths to win me, who honors me with the care of this planet with him, who turns me to all people as brothers and sisters in love, and who uses death as the occasion to usher me into his kingdom.

27. *Death is the Enemy*

I have watched many people die, and death is never pretty.
All the poets of the world, romanticizing it as they will,
have not succeeded in taking from death its hurt. I have
seen the bloody, mangled body of a boy of eight, crushed
by a city bus as he dashed after his ball. I have watched the
emaciated face of a man of 80 as his last gasping breath
failed to come. Despite the smile that seemed to linger on
the lips of the teen-age girl as she slept away, there was no
way for our wearied spirits to feel elation. Death is the
enemy.

Death is universal in human life. Everyone accepts as
natural and obvious that he must die. At the same time, a
secret protest and an inextinguishable sorrow before the end
is a part of every man.

This is not to say that the actual moment of death does
not have its relief. "He died without a struggle"; "Look
how peaceful he seems"; "Now his pain is over." Deep
down, behind and beyond these comforting phrases there
still lies the indignation, the protest, the horror. Life is
right; death is wrong.

It is easier to be reconciled when death comes after a full
and rich life. The man has reared his family, he has finished
his work, the years have ebbed to their end, the energies

have flagged, and the eyes have grown dim. The end comes, and there is no wrenching pain in those who remain behind. But when death strikes a young mother of three, comes like a thief in the night and leaves a distraught husband and father, to be reconciled to death is something else. In either event, however, whether in old or in young, death itself is cruel.

We can regard the rhythm of nature with calm. The green of spring, the rich verdure of summer, the riot of autumn leaves, the deep sleep of winter—these seem to be a perfect sequence. Even with birds and fish and beasts we have little trouble. That fish return to spawn and then to die strikes us with a melancholy beauty. But not man! Shakespeare's celebrated five stages of man leave us utterly disconsolate. For man there should be no death. Death is a savage and horrible intruder into the cycle that belongs to man.

Man is rightly afraid of death. Actually, he should not die. He possesses within him the vitality of a divine life which, if it could assert itself, pure and unveiled, in this earthly life, would eliminate death. He was not created to die. He was created to live on forever. If we are to interpret the repugnance of death as simply a vital, bodily urge for self-preservation, we misunderstand his deeper nature. Like the moaning of a distant sea, the murmuring of eternity within cries out against death. It is not a cry for survival; it is the longing for fulfillment.

Whatever else we glean from reading the first chapters of the Book of Genesis in the Old Testament, it is plain that the Creator did not have death in his design. At the end of each episode of creation, including man as the last, God surveyed what he had done and declared it good. To man was given "the breath of life," the stamp of immortality.

He was created in the image of God, in his likeness. He was to be a companion of God. He was given the gift of freedom, the right of independence, the unique quality which was God's alone. And death was not a part of this divine endowment.

When death did appear on the scene, in the wake of man's estrangement and rebellion against God, God in his love took steps to stage a recovery. Man, created to be deathless, must be recovered for a deathless state.

The strangest and most climactic chapter of the biblical account unfolds around the conquest of death. God sent his Son, in the person of Jesus of Nazareth, and in his death and resurrection death itself was destroyed. Eternal life was reopened for man. Death still ravages the children of men, but death no longer has the last word. When death has done its worst and can do no more, the original dimension of life which God the Creator had designed for him is renewed. Because of Christ, man, though temporarily overcome by death, rises again to a new and deathless life.

There is no way to understand man's deep resistance to death except in the context of this biblical account of man. By all the laws of nature, death should not be horrible. It should be the calm rhythm of man's existence. But man is born to live, not to die. Death remains his hideous, cruel executioner, alien to man and to God.

28. The Bigger Job

His life had not been altogether untroubled. But he had overcome the obstacles. He finished the university with honors. He married a lovely girl. He gained the confidence of his company and went from one promotion to another. At 52 he was "on top of the world." Then his doctor told him he had six months to live.

He had been given many hard assignments in his work. Now he faced the most difficult assignment. How would he meet illness, pain, and death? This was the biggest job he had ever been given.

Would he collapse into self-pity? Would he seethe in anger? Would he let pain make him irritable and bitter? Would he make life miserable for his family, his friends, and for the people who were assigned to care for him? Or would these six months turn out to be the most memorable, perhaps the most cherished of all the months he had lived? They could be.

E. Stanley Jones, the famous missionary, describes an eagle caught in a sudden mountain storm. The fury of the winds threatens to dash the bird against the crags. The bird wheels into the storm, tilts his wings at an angle, and seems to be poised, unmoving in the winds. Gradually the winds lift him up and up until at last he rises above the gale and the crags. The very power that might have destroyed him brings him to calm.

If a man is to succeed in his most arduous assignment, illness and death, he will need to tilt the wings of his spirit in a way that allows him to rise into calm. This is an assignment which requires nobility, charity, patience, and faith. And who knows, maybe these qualities are greater than the drive, the ambition, skill and industry which make a man successful in his earlier, less demanding challenges.

George Macdonald, the British divine and author, pointed out that the Lord does not love a "weary collapse." We are to fight back. Even to capitulate or surrender to his will is not good enough. We are to *embrace* his will. One of the fine gifts our Lord gives is life itself. We are to treasure it. It is given us in trust, day by day, moment by moment. It is no tribute to God to give up the fight to keep it. Even when the verdict is as statistically certain as "six months," we are not to surrender.

Who knows the ultimate mystery of healing? Moreover, even when we are in the most robust of health, we hold the gift of life in an open hand. We have no absolute title to it; we can never keep it by clutching it, but we are to cherish it. We are not to toss it away. There is nothing wrong in hoping against hope for healing until the very moment life is gone. While in college I worked as a night orderly in a hospital. I had never seen anyone die. The nurses told me that this night I would see death; a man in the last stages of cancer couldn't last the night. He did not die, but three weeks later left the hospital and four months later dropped in to tell us he was managing his farm again.

More important than fighting for life itself is to grow in those qualities without which life itself is hardly worth keeping. The Bible calls them "the fruits of the spirit." I

know a man who is crippled by arthritis. I think he is in
constant pain, but his mind at 70 is as sharp as a razor and
his spirit as warm and expansive as the summer sun. He
never begs for sympathy, and every time I am with him I
am cheered. I have known people who realize they very
likely will never leave the hospital alive, but they radiate
such kindness, joy, and concern for others that they shame
and bewilder me. I come to cheer them, and they turn the
tables and cheer me.

We had better be realistic. When pain is there, when one
suddenly faces the likelihood of imminent death, when all
sorts of practical issues may need to be settled, and when
people around the bedside cannot disguise the tragedy they
feel—for the patient to mount a white horse and lead
everyone into the land of courage will require a superhuman
endowment of both patience and faith. But there are superhuman resources at hand. God who himself is on the side of
life and joy will not abandon the hour. He, too, would like
to convert the hour of tragedy into an hour of triumph.
The odds are great, but God is equal to many odds. Given
a chance, he will pour into the arena of sickness and death
resources of grace that we had not dreamed could be there.

And he who is ill has a chance to make the last part of his
life more rich and memorable than any other. He can leave
with his loved ones a legacy of love and courage that will
sustain them in ways that his continued, commonplace life
might not have done. They will understand if he cannot.
They will be eternally grateful if he can.

29. 'It Won't Be Long'

He had surgery six weeks ago—a malignant tumor in the lower abdomen. Returning from the hospital, he had a good week and began supplementary treatments. Last week he was again in the hospital—a threatened obstruction, and more surgery. The cancer has spread. The doctors say it won't be long.

He is my dear friend, in his early sixties. I depend on him as on a brother. His going will leave a large, empty place against the sky.

What now do I say to him? I need not disguise the diagnosis of the surgeon. My friend knows, but I don't want him to give up, whatever the odds. As long as there is life, I believe we are to try to keep it. He is not the kind to capitulate into a "weary collapse." I have reminded him of this. We both know—have known all along—that God's gift of life to us has no sure promise of tenure. We also know that the odds have been wrong, and that terminal illnesses have taken a strange turn and have not been terminal at all. I urge him to fight for life, all the while knowing that if this round is lost, everything is not lost. Both of us believe in a consummate life on the other side. (I have just received the news that he died last night.)

What do I say to his dear wife? Together they have

looked forward to many years when, his arduous work done
and his extensive travels over, they could have a continuity
of companionship which the years have denied them. I can
remind her that she has children and grandchildren to flank
her. I can tell her that her memories are rich, with a mini-
mum of regrets to plague her. She has a profession, and I
can urge her to continue in her work. I can remind her that
she would not want him to live, if his life now had to be
reduced to continuous pain and invalidism. She, too, be-
lieves in heaven, and I can hold before her the eventual
prospect of reunion. None of this will take away the pain
and the loneliness. They have loved one another deeply,
and love will exact its price.

What do I say to myself? I know the truth of Donne's
lines, ". . . ask not for whom the bell tolls; it tolls for
thee." I am less because he is gone. The death of each
friend whittles away another piece of my life. The years
bring on a kind of melancholy, therefore, and mirth is
harder to come by. I comfort myself with the thought that
we had many years at work together, and they were good
years. We might have had many less, or we might not have
known one another at all. And I know that both he and I
are expendable in the work we did together; others can take
our places. I am confident, too, that his work is not lost.
Others will reap the fruits of his efforts.

Another question looms up: Suppose the verdict were
given to me and not to him? How would I deal with myself?
The brave words that I hope may help him—would they
help me? How can I know? I have never faced imminent
death. Try as I do to remind myself that my heart may stop
at any moment, death still has been, if not a remote possi-
bility, at least less than a pressing issue. As a pastor of
twenty years, I have faced death with many other people.

I recognize that when death knocks at my door, it may be different. My hope is that I may face it without panic, and that the faith I have confessed these many years will not fail me.

Life is precious. Another friend of mine who in a heart attack made his journey through the valley of the shadow of death and who recovered to live many good years, once shared a hotel room with me. As we were talking he said, "Al, you will never know how good life is until you are in danger of losing it." Life is precious, not merely because the heart keeps beating, but because of all the dividends that life brings—the love of dear ones, significant work to do, the sun and the sky and the birds. Even when life imposes suffering and pain or tasks that are unpleasant, life is still good.

We ought to get up each morning with a prayer of gratitude, thanking God that we are healthy enough to get out of bed to go and do the things we don't want to do. Upon his retirement, the late Archbishop Fisher of Canterbury said that all through the years he had been able to wake up each morning in glad anticipation of the bad news that the day's mail would bring and that now, losing a bit of the zest for it, he thought he ought to retire.

With all its mixture of mirth and grief, pleasant and unpleasant people, fear and joy, hard tasks and easy ones life still is good.

Now death has overtaken the archbishop. I thank God for the years he was given and the great work he was able to do. I will believe that death's victory is essentially fraudulent, succeeding only in giving the Lord a chance to put him on his feet again in another part of his vast empire.

30. *The Darkest Hour*

This may not be the hour of death. Rather, it may be the knowledge that we must go on living when, for all the world, we don't know why. It may be waking up each morning to another day of nameless fears. It may be falling into restless sleep each night to face in the morning another day of dark moods. The day brings no light. The cheerfulness of people around us only intensifies the darkness that engulfs us. We have no hope. Life itself is a sentence worse than death. We are within the walls of the black prison of life. Death, we hope wistfully, would be a wonderful escape.

We echo the words of Macbeth,

> *Tomorrow and tomorrow and tomorrow*
> *Creep in this petty pace from day to day,*
> *To the last syllable of recorded time:*
> *And all our yesterdays*
> *Have lighted fools the way to dusty death;*
> *Out, out brief candle . . .*

These dark hours come to young and old, poor and rich, unemployed and employed. The man whose day is filled with demanding duties may have them; the man without a job may have them. A high school student with good grades may have them; his grandfather with a life of successful achievement behind him may have them. Sickness and health are no respecter of darkness. It may come to anyone.

There are temporary escapes—drugs, alcohol, plunging with Dionysian passion into the sensuous. But they are temporary distractions, and eventually only deepen the darkness. Sometimes there is help from a friend, a psychiatrist, a pastor.

But suppose the darkness does not disappear. Suffering, whether physical or mental, continues. The future remains an impenetrable fog. Tomorrow may not be better, only worse. Can one learn to live with the darkness, and without despair? Is the darkness itself a necessary part of the whole —some great, mysterious, purposeful whole?

When John Milton, the great poet, became blind, he said, "They also serve who only stand and wait." Within God's great plan of restoring man to his destined glory, is there a place for darkness, for fear, for suffering? Is the pattern of life which was Jesus'—his birth in poverty, his continued poverty, his rejection by family and friends, his loneliness in the Garden of Gethsemane, the darkness of that Friday and the cross—is this a clue to the great plan? If so, when suffering and loneliness and fear come to us, are they more than something to correct or escape? Are they something to endure, and in enduring them (and not escaping them) are we serving the larger and more mysterious plan that God has for redeeming the world? Certainly God wants to give us joy and hope and exuberance for life, but if that does not happen, then what? Are we lost to God's more comprehensive purposes for mankind, or does our very suffering fit somewhere, like a significant piece in the large jigsaw puzzle of God?

Some suffering, of course, clearly comes from misdirected or sinful behavior. A man languishes in prison because he murdered someone. A man becomes ill because of overindulgence in liquor or food. But there is a vast area of suffering which follows no pattern of cause and effect. It simply comes. Darkness descends. Courage fades. Fears surge around. All efforts of friends or physicians fail. Even prayer doesn't help. The future is gray. How can we go on living?

The Apostle Paul had such an hour. He prayed God to deliver him from "the thorn in the flesh," whatever that was. God's reply was simply, "My grace is sufficient." Apparently Paul lived with this darkness, this suffering, his whole life through. It may have been important for him personally; it may also have been a thread in the larger fabric of God's work on earth. Who knows? It could very well be.

God grooms us for his own kingdom. He is busy, through the Holy Spirit, shaping us to be the kind of people who can inhabit this kingdom. This "basic training" of man may involve the whole gamut of fears and sufferings. To leave us undisciplined, always doing, willy-nilly, what we like to do, enjoying only the brightness and never knowing darkness, may leave us totally unprepared for the glories of the kingdom.

In a profound sense, God is not the author of the dark hours. It was his intention to have man in unbroken, joyous companionship with him. But sin and tragedy and death came in through the back door. To redeem man, to restore what was lost, God uses the very darkness that was not of his doing. The black pieces are woven into the bright pieces in the totality of the divine jigsaw puzzle. Suffering and joy are inseparable in the whole. The blind man who only sits and waits also serves the purposes of God. The arthritic who will never leave his bed also serves. How, we do not know, but in the great providence of God, suffering has a place and a role.

31. I Want to Live

I want to live. I don't want to die.

I love the scudding clouds, the blazing sunset, the laughter of a child, the touch of my lover's hand.

Life is good. Even on dark days, life is still good. I do not want to let it go.

I may have to let it go. My car may careen on a slippery pavement, and I may be on my way to the morgue. Cancer may strike its capricious blow, and the doctor walk silently from my room. A bomb may drop from the sky. The atmosphere may cloud over with civilization's pollutions and rob me of breath. Life is uncertain, I know, but I still want to live.

Life always has been uncertain. In many parts of the earth, less than half the children survive birth. The median age for death is 30. In earlier civilizations, death was around the corner for everyone. Death is no stranger to our world. But I still want to live.

Despite the vast resources of modern medicine, our modern world is haunted by the prospect of death. Never has the promise of individual survival been brighter; never has the prospect of corporate survival been darker. Ever since the development of the atom bomb, the fear of gigantic destruction has been a continuing anxiety.

Franz Werfel has described the plight of modern man in the parable of the camel driver who is being pursued by his maddened camel. To escape he leaps into a well. Falling, his clothes catch on a root in the wall of the well. There he hangs, suspended. Looking up, he sees the glowering eyes of his enraged camel. Looking down, he sees the fiery eyes of a dragon. And as his eyes become accustomed to the light he sees two mice, one white, the other black, taking alternate bites at the base of the root. A very nasty situation.

Mr. Werfel says that man had thought to be the driver of the machine, but that the machine, gone mad, threatens to destroy him. Meantime, he faces on the one hand the fury of the ungovernable machine (the camel), and on the other hand the prospect of some catastrophic death (the dragon). In this moment time is running out, day and night (the white mouse and the black mouse). This, Mr. Werfel says, is the mood of modern man.

It is true that never before has the world entertained destruction on such a colossal scale. It is equally true that never before has man had the resources of power and technical knowledge to solve so many of its problems. Every problem—hunger, war, overpopulation, pollution—is within reach of solution. Man has the skills. The world of tomorrow could be vastly better than any period of the earth's history.

We need no new knowledge, not even more wisdom. We do need the *will* to live. There must be more than the individual will to live, each to himself. We must want to live together, corporately, as one great, human family upon the earth. Nothing short of this kind of will can deliver the exciting promises for tomorrow.

Our Christian faith releases us for limitless hope. With God all things are possible. He must love this earth and its possibilities to send his Son to become a part of its hurts and to surmount its tragedies with a resurrection from the dead. How can I, then, limit the promise for the tomorrow?

And the promise is here. The ominous clouds of possible doom are pierced by shafts of light. There are signs of hope. Vast parts of the world that have lived in unchanging drudgery for centuries are stirring with anticipation of a new day. People who have been frozen into groups, generation after generation, are breaking out of their mold, and claiming the rights of man. The "have nations" are awakening to their responsibility for the "have nots." I want to live to be a part of what may become the world's finest hour.

Whatever the outcome for the world, I want to live for today—for each day, as the days come and go. I like the wind in the treetops, the song of birds, even the roar of the turbine. I exult in the restless curiosity of man that ferrets out the secrets of nature. I am moved to tears by the soaring crescendos of a symphony, or the tender plucking of a guitar. The world is full of beauty, in color, form, and music. And people—some good and some bad, the good and the bad in each of us. I like people. I want to live to enjoy them. I do not want to die.